Think of Little Things

Published by **Sendpoints IPS Co., Ltd.** Publisher **Gengli Lin** Chief Editor **Nicole Lo**
Design Director **Nicole Lo** Designer **Ruosong Liao, Amy Lee** Executive Editors **Joann Zhong, Virginia Ruan, Catherin Huang** Editorial Desk **editorial@brandmagazine.com.hk**
Inquiries **Zebin Yao**
T: +86-20-89095121-8043
E: ad@brandmagazine.com.hk (*Advertising*)
E: marketing@brandmagazine.com.hk (*Collaboration*)
Distribution Manager **Kris Guo**
T: +86-20-81007895
E: sales@sendpoints.cn Address **Flat/Rm 4, 5/F, Tak Lee Building, 270-280 Queens Road West, Hong Kong**
T: +852-69502452
F: +852-35832448
E: info@brandmagazine.com.hk
Website **www.brandmagazine.com.hk**
ISSN **2226-6542**
International Distributors **UK**
Central Books
T: + 44 845 458 9925
F: + 44 845 458 9912
Arnolfini Books
T: + 44 117 9172306
F: + 44 117 9172303
Artwords Bookshop
T: + 44 20 7729 2000
F: + 44 20 7729 4400
Charlotte Street News
T: + 44 20 7636 4270
F: + 44 20 7419 7490
Fat Buddha Ltd
T: + 44 141 226 8972
Foyles
T: + 44 20 7440 3265
EUROPE ONLINE SUBSCRIPTIONS
Centralbooks
www.centralbooks.com
Newsstand
www.newsstand.co.uk
Pineapple Media
T: + 44 2392 787970
www.pineapple-media.com

Cover illustration by Nimura Daisuke (Japan)

ICA Bookshop
  T: + 020 7930 3647
Germany
Do You Readme?! GbR [Berlin]
  T: + 0049 30 695 49 695
  F: + 0049 30 695 49 696
Amsterdam
Athenaeum Boekhandel
  T: + 00 31 20 622 6248
  F: + 00 31 20 638 4901
Poland
Muzeum Sztuki Nowoczesnej
  W Warszawie
Ireland
Books Upstairs
  T: + 353 1 677 8566
Norway
Interpress Norge AS
  T: + 47 225 73241
Portugal
In Uteis Design LDA [Lisbon]
  T: + 351 225 088 474
  F: + 351 225 088 475
Sweden
Svenska Interpress AB
  T: + 46 8 506 506 00
USA
Disticor Magazine Distribution
Services
  T: + 1 905- 619-6565
Daily News
  T: + 7811155507
Chile
GONZALO OSORIO PETIT
  T: + 56 32 2397498
  F: + 56 32 2397498

Australia
Beautiful Pages
  T: + (02) 9356 2331
Mag Nation
  T: + 61 03 9663 6559
Readings Pty Ltd
  T: + 03 9347 6633
New Zealand
NATIONWIDE BOOK DISTRIBUTORS
  T: + +64 3 312 1603
Korea
Hong-ik Designbook
  T: + 82 2 333 0346
Japan
NIPPAN IPS CO., LTD
  T: +81 3 5842 9050
Malaysia/Singapore/Indonesia
Basheer Graphic
  T: + 60 2 713 2236
Thailand
Asia Books Co., Ltd
  T: + 662 715 9000
India
SBD Subscription Services
  T: + 91 11 2871 4138
China
Sendpoints Books Co., Ltd [Mainland]
  T: +86-20-89095121-8007
Multi-Arts Corporation [Taiwan]
  T: + 886 2 2505 2288
The Eslite Culture Hong Kong Limited
[Hong Kong]
  T: + 852 3419 6789

BRAND

Think of Little Things

issue
43

AD
Art Director
CD
Creative Director
D
Designer
DS
Design Studio
DA
Design Agency
P
Photographer
Ill
Illustrator
CL
Client
CW
Copywriter

EDITORIAL

You know what?
You are
the most magical little thing
on earth!

Nicole Lo
Editor-in-Chief

anDISCOVERY©

anDIRECTION©

Brandesign®

1
In
Dialogues with
DOIY ,
Marina Willer &
Nakagawa Masashichi Shoten

2
Out
Dialogues with
Joe Fang ,
Helen Downie &
Nimura Daisuke

1

We all like things that are nice-looking, user-friendly and fun. When we stay at home or indoors, we often expect the company of something interesting to spend the rare leisure time. Delicious food, household supplies that are simple and easy on the eyes, lovely and surprising toys and games, cards, little accessories and the like are the "little things" which produce pleasure and happiness in our busy life filled with trifles. With our eyes, ears, tongues, noses and hands, we gain feelings straightforward to soul, fulfilling or placating our sentiments. Either a soft towel, condiment dish dipping to show the shapes in different phases of the moon, or a warm scented candle, bright-colored toy, a little thing with good design is never disappointing in pacifying our hearts.

Dialogue with DOIY

DOIY

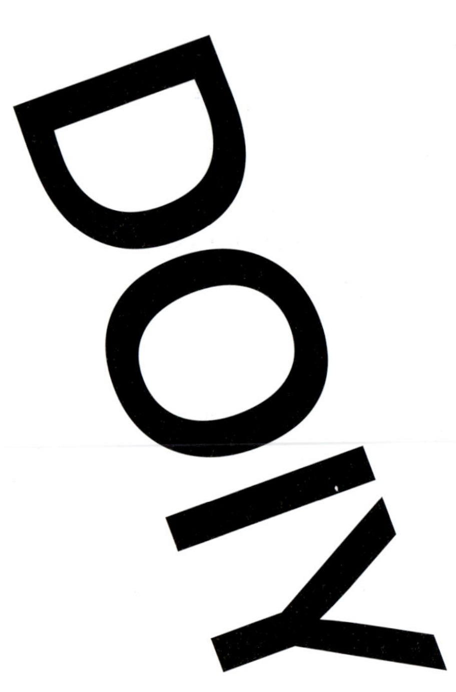

DOIY was born out of an alchemy between people seeking the same playful, intriguing, creative challenge. Elodie's restless creative mind and Jaime's search for beauty and perfectionism found themselves together in 2008.

Different soil breeds different flowers. On the passionate earth of Spain, spark of the collision between multiple cultures and their strong artistic atmosphere gives birth to diverse design, with either humorous amusements or quiet magnificence. In a time when normcore and Nordic Style prevail, DOIY, a brand rooted in the fascinating city of Barcelona, steps on an extraordinary way. DOIY, i.e., Do It Yourself. The brand turns design into a symbol of felicity, to make our daily life more fun.

What products have their souls? For Elodie and Jaime, founders of DOIY, homewares on the market are uninteresting without souls. Elodie has numerous ideas and thoughts while Jaime is a strict perfectionist. The couple initiated their collaboration in Barcelona and embarked on a path seeking and creating interesting products.

Invested with the couple's ideas, DOIY will never keep to the beaten track. Creativeness, surprises and little excitements are perfectly incubated in the founders' wonderful partnership, and thus is born the brand DOIY. For DOIY, there is no restrictions on function and shape. Constantly challenging the definition of products, their designers blur the boundaries between trend and function, aesthetics and fun, material and shape, facilitating an appropriate fusion of art and design. In the Hestia series, pillars in ancient temples coming down from on high are transformed into scented candles; the many Greek heroes and goddesses walk to the dining-table and share food with you, transcending to the centu-

Editor & Interviewer
Catherin Huang

DO IT YOURSELF

ries-old brilliant Greek culture. In life too many ideas hover in our mind failing to be put into practice. Why not take a look at the compilation poster from DOIY-100 Things You Must do Before You Die? Or try the 30 Day Challenge card box by ripping down one small card a day and accomplish a small goal according to its instructions, striving to turn life into the way you expect it to be through every trifle. Details of real life being its ceaseless source of inspiration, DOIY creates unique products with playfulness and wit, bringing Easter eggs to life.

It's always been DOIY's design principle to provide services for all. In their eyes, design shall not stand high above the masses. It should appeal to ordinary people and be affordable instead. Creative designs at alluring prices rapidly make DOIY a popular brand in a few years. Now it has reached more than 30 countries covering metropolis such as New York, Tokyo and Paris.

Elodie and Jaime are the co-founders of DOIY. How did you get to know each other and decide to found the corporation? I heard that Jaime is a very strict perfectionist. Can you cite some examples?
We met in the UK in 2003. We first fell in love and second decided to create a business together.
We are both hard-workers, passionate about design and full of enthusiasm. We were seeking the same playful and creative challenge. It was in Barcelona in 2008, when during an improvised late-night conversation our fate came in. Against the picturesque backdrop of a tiny Spanish apartment, we decided to use our creativity, youth, and energy to shape something together. It didn't take too long: the next morning we quitted our jobs.
Jaime is definitely a perfectionist. No defect can pass in front of his eyes without being detected. He foresees any potential future problems that the design could bring up even before anything is even on the table. From the materials, to the packaging, goings through dimensional finishings, every detail has to stop by Jaime's quality customs before going ahead.

DOIY delivers very fresh and novel design with originality, which has quite a lot to do with Elodie's creativity. When did Elodie realize your ideas can change people's life?
"See things differently."
"Don't take anything for granted."
"Who said it had to be this way?"
"Why not turn the concept upside down?"
This is basically how we think. We love to surprise and to be surprised. That's why, when designing, from the initial concept to the design process, everything is simply different, which makes the whole story more playful and original.

It's been a decade since the establishment of DOIY. Are you satisfied with its development? Can you share some experience and insights for starting a business?
These last 10 years have been amazing and when we look back today at what we have created, we are actually very happy. It's been tons of smiles, surprises, good news and fun. There have been also many bumps in the road and a crazy amount of hard work. Products to create, ideas to realize, markets to build, mountains to climb, and for god's sake - staying sane! But one thing is for sure, the journey was never boring.
When you start a business you absolutely need illusion, but illusion is not enough to make it happen. You need to be ready to work, a lot, I mean A LOT. Be ready for success but also for failure. You must not be scared, of anything. You must trust in your dream and make it your priority.

The market has always been evolving. How do you determine the products you develop?
We are passionate about trends, fashion, art and anything related to pop culture. We are naturally interested by anything happening around us. All this contemporary cultural background is always in our mind when we create products.

As a brand open for cooperation, DOIY has had crossover cooperation with a lot photographers, art directors and designers. In what way do you locate and select your collaborators?
We are very connected to the creative scene of Barcelona. We find great artists in events, online, through great talents we know, etc. Barcelona is a great spot to feature emerging talents.

CD
Elodie Deviras & Jaime Monfort

DS
DOIY Design

2018

CACTUS SOCKS

Fun and comfy pair of socks shaped as a cactus.

CD
Elodie Deviras & Jaime Monfort

DS
DOIY Design

2018

HANDY

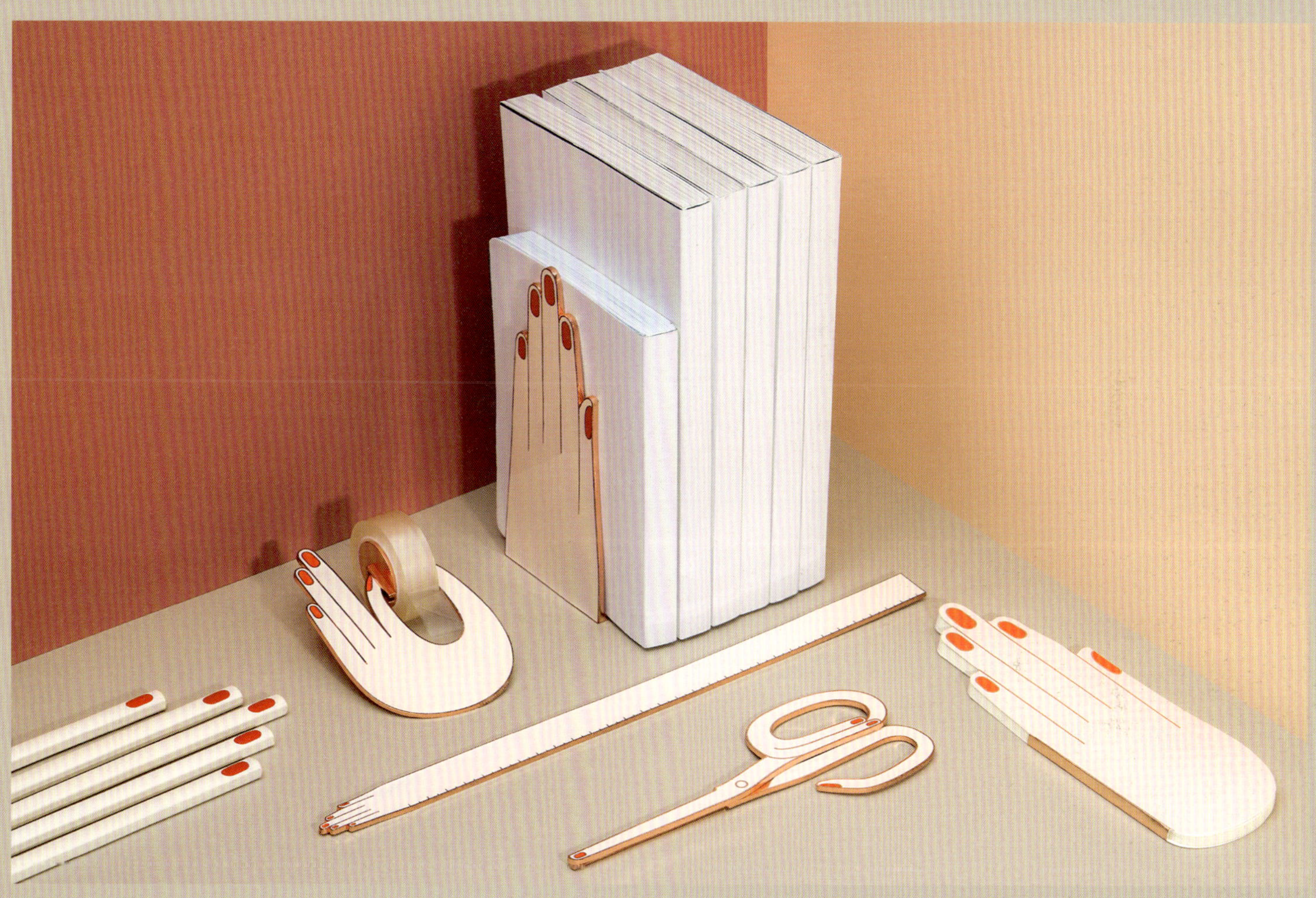

Trendy set of bookends, rulers and notebooks, shaped as hands with painted red nails.

CD
Elodie Deviras & Jaime Monfort

DS
DOIY Design

2018

UNBORING

Quirk and trendy resin paperweights are functional and give your desk a touch of fun.

CD
Elodie Devi
DS
DOIY Design

2018

ORGANS

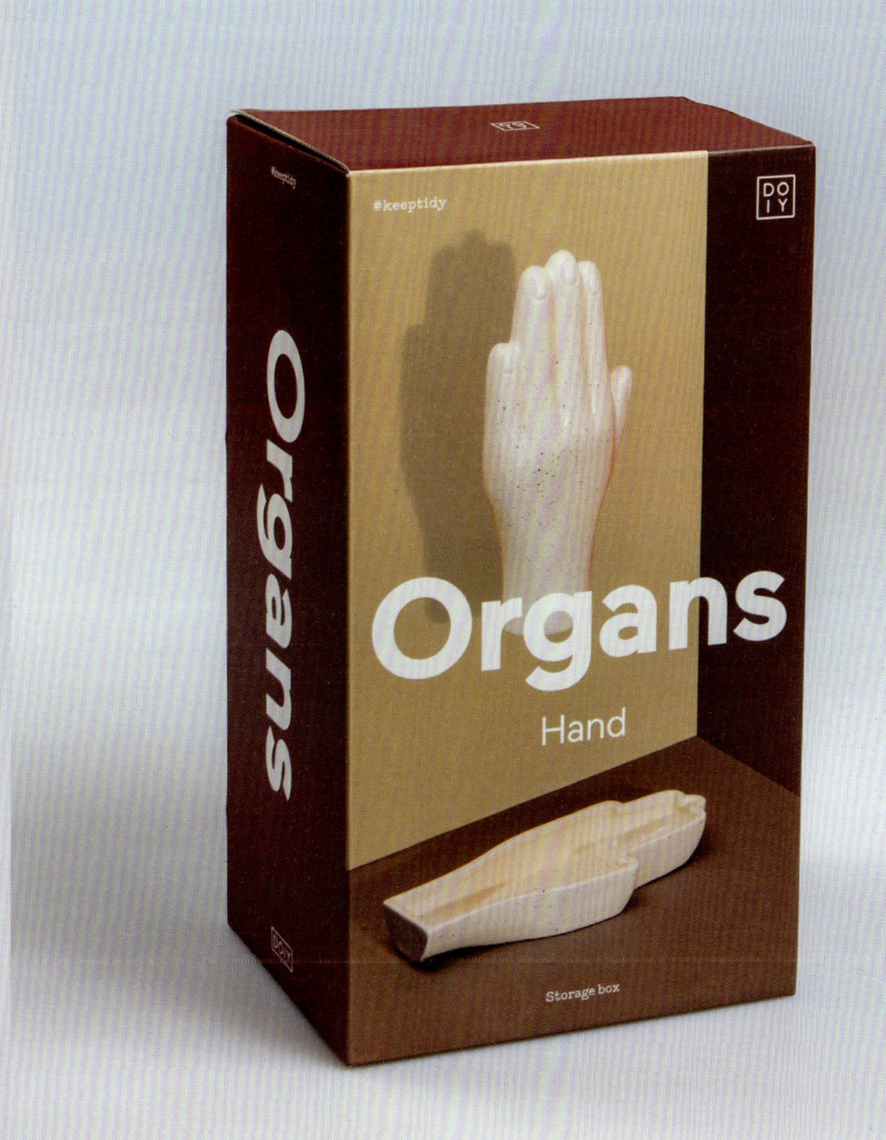

Modernity at its finest, these ceramic handcrafted storage boxes with flecked finishing feature human organs.

CD
Elodie Deviras & Jaime Monfort

DS
DOIY Design

2018

SUZANNE SAROFF

Just as the photographer Suzanne Saroff distorts reality through Hestia glassware, DOIY gives a new meaning, an alternative reality to its objects.

IN
SAGUARO GLASSES & CARAFE
CD
Elodie Deviras & Jaime Monfort
DS
DOIY Design
2018
Set of glass carafe and 6 stackable glasses recreate a saguaro cactus once piled up.
It is decorative, surprising and useful for any home.

KOINOBORI

Travel cotton laundry bag shaped as a "Koinobori" (mythical Japanese carp-shaped wind sock) is a very handy travel mate thanks to its perfect hand-luggage size.

CD
Elodie Deviras & Jaime Monfort

DS
DOIY Design

2018

Dialogue with MARINA WILLER

Marina Willer

Marina Willer is a graphic designer and film-maker with an MA in Graphic Design from the Royal College of Art. Before joining Pentagram as a partner, she was the head creative director for Wolff Olins in London. During the course of her career, Willer has led the design of major identities schemes for Amnesty International, Tate, Southbank Centre, Serpentine Galleries, Oxfam, Nesta, Second Home and Sam Labs, among many others.

Founded in 1972, the design firm Pentagram is more like a design alliance. Its predecessor was "Fletcher & Forbes" founded by Alan Fletcher and Colin Forbes in the end of the 1950s. In the years that followed, they included several partners and added their names to the company name. But in 1972, they decided to abandon personal names and adopt "Pentagram" instead, and began to focus on graphic, architectural and industrial design. With equality as the basic principle for its collaborative relations, Pentagram only accepts designers who have gained some fame in the design industry. Every member of the company is its partner, and without administrative staff and board of directors, everyone is allowed to independently handle financial transactions.

Its partners are respectively responsible for their own design team and projects, but can fulfill clients' special needs by virtue of the force and resources from the other partners. The founders believe their clients will benefit from their interdisciplinary design solutions integrating various inspirations and skills, since this integration allows designs to maintain originality and develop. This strategy has been proved to be successful and helped the firm to grow as the world's top design alliance. Clients have come with design questions, because they believe that Pentagram's design solutions are generally the best, though not always the safest or most traditional.

Editor
Virginia Ruan

The Best Interdisciplinary Design Solutions

Interviewer
Virginia Ruan

Each client or project has different needs and we need to respond to them but also push clients when they need to be challenged to achieve what they need.

Pentagram was founded in 1972 on the premise of collaborative interdisciplinary designers working together in an independently owned firm of equals. How many branches and partners do you have now? How does the organization function?
We have London, NY, Austin and Berlin. Each partner looks after their own team, both creatively and financially. We each have targets to make and the pressure to make amazing work. We don't interfere with each other's methods. We just share inspiration and support from being together. We collaborate when needed or relevant. All partners earn the same salary.

How does the company choose its partners?
Each partner forms a team from zero, we hire each member of our teams. It's mostly creative with a little bit of support from Project Management.

Has any project or person challenged how you think about graphic design in recent years?
Yes. All the time. We have to stay relevant. Each client or project has different needs and we need to respond to them but also push clients when they need to be challenged to achieve what they need. All members of my team bring new perspectives and challenge things by doing that.

How do you think online design resources have influenced the graphic design being produced today?
The world has become addicted to technology. That can bring opportunities and challenges. Behaviour is changing; attention span is short; the understanding of reality is confronted with too much being experienced purely online. But that makes us have to work harder to create meaningful experiences and connections. Not just bombard the world with more distraction.

What are you currently fascinated by and how is it feeding into your work?

I am interested in change. How we can create design systems that can adjust with change. That can embrace the constant movement and still remain coherent with certain principles.

Do you have a hobby of collecting something? If yes, what would you like to collect and why?
I love mapping and doodling ideas, words and thoughts. Collecting, organising and disorganising them to create stories and mind maps. That is good to keep the mind sane and to do things by hands, to remain tactile.

PIGZBE

D
Filippo Yacob, Jon Marshall &
David Jakes

DS
Pigzbe & Pentagram

P
Roger Stillman

2018

Pigzbe is a fintech start-up that helps children and their families learn the principles of 21st century finance through cryptocurrency savings and hands-on play. It does this through a handheld "Piggy-Wallet" and an educational app, which are powered by a new digital currency called "Wollo".
The design team's aim was to provide a tangible interface to digital money, working as a 21st century replacement for the traditional piggy bank. The Pigzbe device is a connected product which works as a notifier, controller and storage device for digital currency. Its LED matrix display communicates notifications and messages and an integrated speaker and vibration motor enhance the user experience with sound and haptics while an accelerometer allows motion and gestures to be used, such as shaking the device to check the balance.
The physical device integrates closely with the Pigzbe App that lets the whole family send money to a child's Pigzbe from anywhere in the world instantly and securely. For kids, the App is a playful interface for more advanced activities, like setting savings goals, learning about budgeting, sharing and spending. For parents, the app is an easy way to engage with your children's financial education.

NAKAGAWA MASASHICHI SHOTEN

Wander with

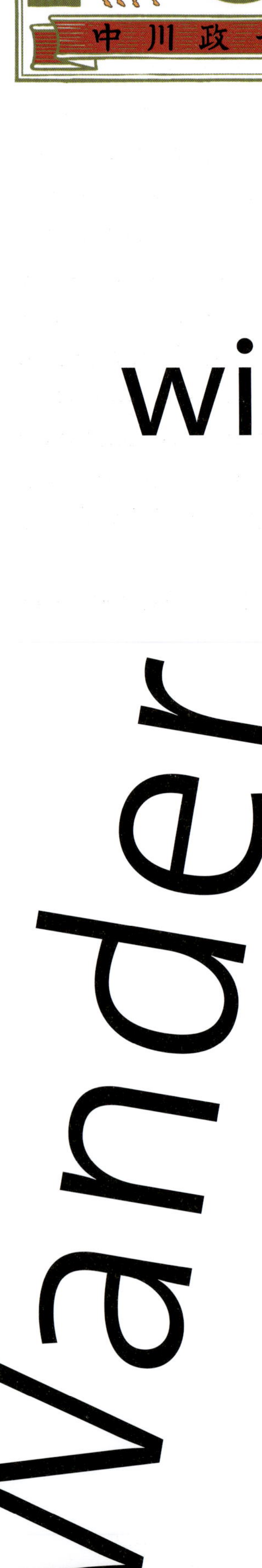

**Nakagawa Masashichi
Shoten Co., Ltd.**

An evolving traditional company which has applied know-how to start the project of revitalizing traditional Japanese crafts. It uses its knowledge of consultation in specialized market style and specialized distribution route for household goods market as well as its ability in brand management to the fullest, which it has achieved through its own brands, to create many "regional No.1s" and revitalize traditional Japanese crafts.

Having been flourishing everywhere in our country, Muji may have grown to be a brand representing Japanese lifestyle. But actually, keeping an eye on zakka stores for Japanese lifestyle, we will spot another brand comparable with Muji - Nakagawa Masashichi Shoten Co., Ltd. ("Nakagawa Masashichi Shoten" for short), a long standing brand which has stores in downtown areas of various Japanese cities.

Founded in 1716, how does this 3 century-old store balance the changed and unchanged in strategy in this modern commercial world when people are calling for carrying forward the precious traditions of the nation? Natsumi Sato responsible for the company's Public Relations told *BranD* that Nakagawa Masashichi Shoten has always kept a vision of "Revitalizing Japanese Crafts" which is the foundation of its strength. Starting from a small shop selling Nara Hemps, Nakagawa Masashichi Shoten set its headquarter in Japan's ancient Nara Prefecture. The fine handmade linen fabric Nara Hemp was listed among the supplies for Tokugawa during the Shogunate Period. In 1898, it even became one of the imperial supplies and was exhibited in the Universal Exposition to represent Japan's local conditions. Traditional handicrafts, however, are destined to go downfall once outpaced by the times. Like other century-old stores, Nakagawa Masashichi Shoten has stumbled over the years. Due to its complicated production process and high prices, Nara Hemp has gradually been knocked out in modern times and the enterprise was confronted with business distress for a time.

In 2008, Nakagawa Jun became the 13th president of Nakagawa Masashichi Shoten and

Editor
Virginia Ruan

Reactivated Old Brand

began to make substantial reforms. From a small struggling sunset firm in Kyoto, Nakagawa Masashichi Shoten rapidly grew into a trendy brand of Japanese daily goods. It became not only the essential brand in dozens of Japan's large shopping malls, but also the representative of Japanese zakka stores. One of the must-gos for tourists now, the company now has 55 stores in Japan, bagging an annual business turnover of more than JPY¥5,700 million.

Born in 1974, Nakagawa Jun graduated from School of Law, Kyoto University and once worked for Fujitsu. After taking charge of the company, he innovated the traditional handicrafts and adjusted the company's management styles and brand strategy, increasing a lot retail stores all over Japan and establishing developed online sales network. More importantly, he put a lot of efforts into the store design. He invited famous designer Manabu Mizuno to design for the store space, product visual and multi-media for the brand, renovating its image. Manabu Mizuno thinks that Nara Prefecture has a history longer than that of Kyoto and has a richer ancient atmosphere. The company's long history and its home Nara are great assets and advantages of Nakagawa Masashichi Shoten. He adopted the philosophy of "new discovery in old things" and wove it into the overall product development and design. Thus, the brand was endowed with a temperament of more Japanese and folkloric native culture.

By virtue of this rebranding, Nakagawa Jun led the team onto the road of ceaseless innovation and developed multiple new brands. In the interview, Sato revealed with the reform the company began to roll out a wider variety of self-run zakka brands, including medium and high-end cotton and linen fabric brand Yu Nakagawa, zakka brand Nakagawa Masashichi Shoten focusing on tools for living, Japanese souvenir brand Nipponichi, factory brand for socks "2&9" and handkerchief brand "Motta" etc.

In Nakagawa Jun's eyes, the power of brand is significant, so he wants to attract new consumer groups by changing the original brand image. That's why he focuses on brand expansion. Nakagawa Masashichi Shoten originally had only one brand Yu Nakagawa. The brand presents textile in mixture of materials, skills, and design which has been passed along in Japan from long ago, and adding an essence of modernity with it. Its target is housewives in Japan.

Nakagawa Jun deems a-sole-brand mode will sooner or later put the company at high risks. In order to reduce risk, he founded the second brand Kisara in 2003. Japan has the traditional etiquette of giving gifts at visits and farewells. Well-positioned since it was created, the brand aims to provide beautiful day-to-day living things that can be gifts for the important ones, things that blend traditional Japanese materials with life of the day, creatively with origami as the packaging, to pass on the spirit of ritual unique in Japan.

In 2010, Nakagawa Jun released Nakagawa Masashichi Shoten, the company's third comprehensive brand. Its remarkable difference from the other two lies in its down-to-earth nature. Focusing on the most daily living tools, it eyes on traditional handicrafts and extract new elements to make things integrating functionality and good looks for ordinary family and life.

Nakagawa Jun's boldness and strategy won him a good reputation, and meanwhile bring about new possibilities to old Japanese creation shops facing collapse like Nakagawa Masashichi Shoten did. So they began to value the reshaping of brands and came to Nakagawa Jun for help. According to Sato, it was then that Nakagawa Masashichi Shoten started its operation consultancy business in its vision to revitalize Japanese crafts. Ever since 2009, the consultant services it has provided to up to 20 old Japanese creation shops have been quite a success, which makes it a "troubleshooter" for Japanese handicraft industry. They don't only treat "Revitalizing Japanese Crafts" as a slogan, but hope that they can exist all the time with their industry.

They don't only treat "Revitalizing Japanese Crafts" as a slogan, but hope that they can exist all the time with their industry.

Sato said the company has a design team to develop original products. The staff have developed good lively relationships, harmonious just like their products. More than anything, all of their employees have a favor for Japanese crafts, living, or "monozukuri" (manufacturing). And they want very much to keep these things as well as the spirits carried in their own life. So they use the company's products in daily life and would exchange user experience at official meetings.

In the decade of revolutionary development, Nakagawa Masashichi Shoten skillfully and flexibly reactivates its brand symbiotic power to maintain a long standing position. "Staying true to the mission" is becoming a cliché. But few enterprises manage to truly practice it and forge ahead. Nakagawa Masashichi Shoten is a mirror that most worth fathoming and pondering.

KUTANIYAKI DISH

CD
Nakagawa Masashichi Shoten

DS
Nakagawa Masashichi Shoten

2018

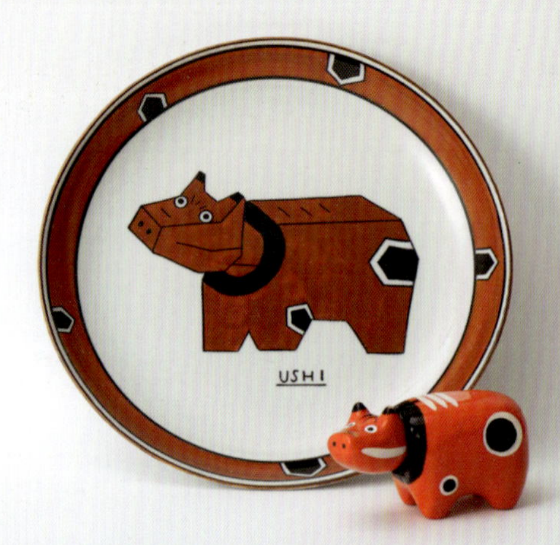

Philippe Weisbecker is a French artist famous for his unique handmade pencil drawings and has a keen interest on Japanese native toys. Born after the Edo period, native toys have been the granted goods for temples and shrines' rituals, specialties and festive presents. Since 2017, Weisbecker has been working with Nakagawa Masashichi Shoten to visit native toy workshops across Japan and create everyday tools with their traditional techniques. Therein, he created 12 original drawings in the center of the Kutaniyaki big dishes, the representative crafted procelain of Ishikawa Prefecture. To represent the colors of the original drawings, the craftsmen tried to make new colors by blending pigments and painted them one by one. These images have also been used to make other series of Japanese native toys.

HITSUJI
WEISBECKER
生地ふきん
INOSHISHI
NEZUMI
TORI
HITSUJI
USHI

SUMMER GREETING CARD

IN

AD & CD
Minoru Dodo

D & Ill
Ayaka Funata

DS
DODO DESIGN

2016

It is a summer greeting card of TAKEO Co., Ltd. which is a paper trading company.
When it arrived, it was simply a postcard, but turning over the picture surface made it a pool where women and mermaids appeared to play.
Taking advantage of the paper material called "Mermaid" with unevenness like undulations on the surface, the paper was looked at as a water surface.
Designers aimed for a card that makes the recipient feel refreshed on the summer day when the harsh heat continues.

D
Kengo Kuma

CD
More Trees Design, Inc.

P
Ikunori Yamamoto & Keisuke Ono

2015

TSUMIKI

TSUMIKI, which means building blocks in Japanese, is simple triangle-shaped wooden blocks designed by a renowned architect Kengo Kuma in collaboration with a forest conservation organization More Trees founded by a musician Ryuichi: Sakamoto.
Inspired by the silhouette of coniferous trees, TSUMIKI's simple triangular shape with architectural features allows itself to be not only a toy encouraging children to develop their flexible creativity but a small star-shaped object art and a superb decoration on walls. It is recommended as baby gifts, shop decorations, or for a wide variety of any other purposes along with people's imagination go. Designers hope people enjoy the warm feeling of this wood product in daily life.
Tsumiki is made of FSC (Forest Stewardship Council) certified cedar from Morotsuka village in Miyazaki prefecture where one of More Trees' forests locates and made by the hands of local skilled artisans.

D
Xiangrong Chen, ANGUS
CHIANG & Yixun Jiang

CD
ANGUS CHIANG & Yixun
Jiang

DS
ANGUS CHIANG

P
Kecheng Lin, James &
ANGUS CHIANG team

2018

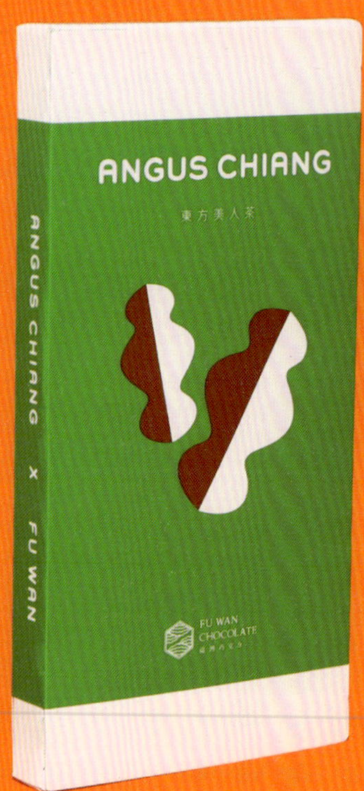

FU WAN CHOCOLATE X ANGUS

To echo the theme of "ANGUS CHIANG" 2019 AW new series, "BACK AT ONE", and deeply explore the characteristics of Taiwan's primary industry of agriculture, forestry, fishing and animal husbandry, Warren Xu, founder of Fu Wan Chocolate, integrated local food materials into the four sectors and designed Oriental Beauty Tea chocolate for agriculture, emperor coffee chocolate for forestry, Chiayi flower of salt chocolate for fishing and Pingtung vanilla chocolate for animal husbandry. Collaborating with designer Hsian Jung Chen, the team simplified the figurative outlines of food materials, applied them to fashion show dress and made abstracted geometric collaborative packaging boxes, interpreting and delivering a different perspective and tribute to the primary industry in a colorful and playful way.

ANGUS CHIANG
X
FU WAN CHOCOLATE
福灣 巧克力
ANGUS CHIANG
ANGUS CHIANG
ANGUS CHIANG
ANGUS CHIANG

AD & CD
BentukBentuk

D
Shahfiq Manap
& Adesh Zaini

DS
BentukBentuk

P
BentukBentuk

2018

FOURSTEPS CARD HOLDER

BENTUKBENTUK

With the aim to change the perception of concrete from a cold and lifeless material, BentukBentuk has infused warmth and brought life into the concrete pieces with stylish yet functional design, suitable for any space. The brand name "BentukBentuk" means "staying true to the root" in Malaysian national language, representing the founders' aesthetics.
Founded in April 2016 by married duo Shahfiq and Adesh after months of countless experiments, BentukBentuk has emerged as one of the leading names in concrete artisanal products in Malaysia.

VORMEN LAMP 2.0 WITH
WOODEN BASE FROM ADIAIDAREKA

POINTY POT

DIP NIGHT

AD, CD & D
Soon Wook Yeom

DS
Actor Design

P
Soon Wook Yeom

2016

This design is based on the moon shape and it is used as a small dish for soy sauce. When this dish is full of soy sauce, it looks like a crescent moon. As the volume of soy sauce begins to decrease, it becomes more similar to a full moon.

AD, CD & D
Soon Wook Yeom

DS
Actor Design

P
Soon Wook Yeom

2017

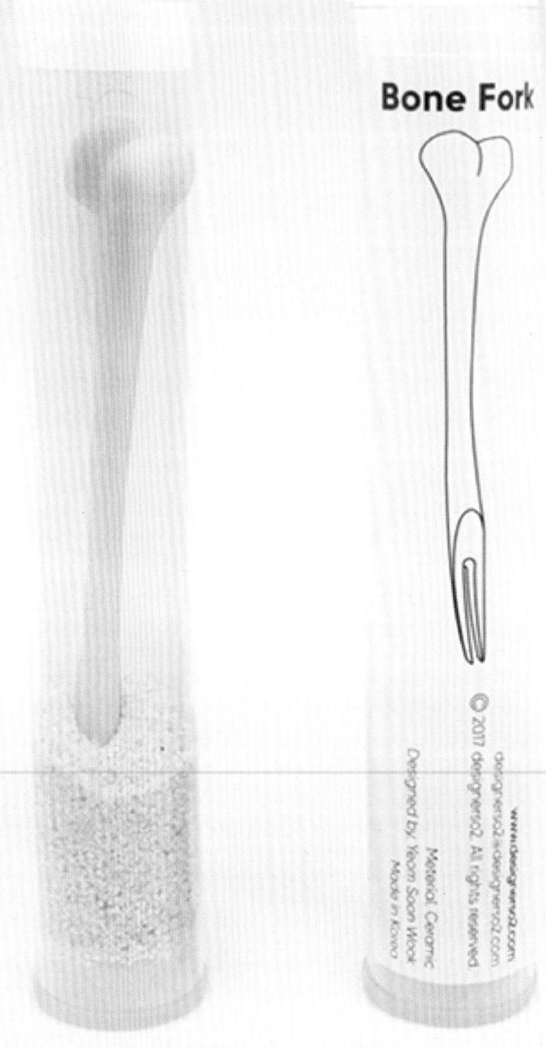

BONE FORK

This design was inspired by primitive people's eating meat, and users of this product can enjoy eating a variety of foods such as fruits and chicken.

WOODEN TOY PACKAGING

D
Can Yang

P
Can Yang

2017

BREAD & BUTTER TOASTER SET's core value is to provide a launch pad to ignite imagination and a sense of wonder in all children so they can discover themselves, their
passions, and their purpose.
In order to fit the brand's image, designer designed all the patterns and graphics in a
friendly pastel palette. The whole packaging consists of a wooden case (which includes
a laser-cut pop-out paddle board), a piece of wrapping fabric, a handle, a manual with
instructions and a keychain as an extra gift. All the materials are environmental-
ly-friendly and serve a second function other than being part of the packaging.

MANUAL
AGES

CD
Ty Mattson

D
Ty Mattson, Kortney
Greer, Luke Bott &
Russ Gray

DS
Mattson Creative

2016-Current

FAO SCHWARZ REBRAND

Renowned for its premium toy collection and legendary in-store experience, FAO Schwarz has been delighting customers for more than 150 years. After the flagship location in New York City closed its doors in 2016, the storied toy retailer came under new ownership and Mattson Creative was hired to revive and revitalize the iconic brand. The result is a visual identity system that honors the brand's remarkable legacy and looks forward to inspiring a new generation of kids...and kids at heart.

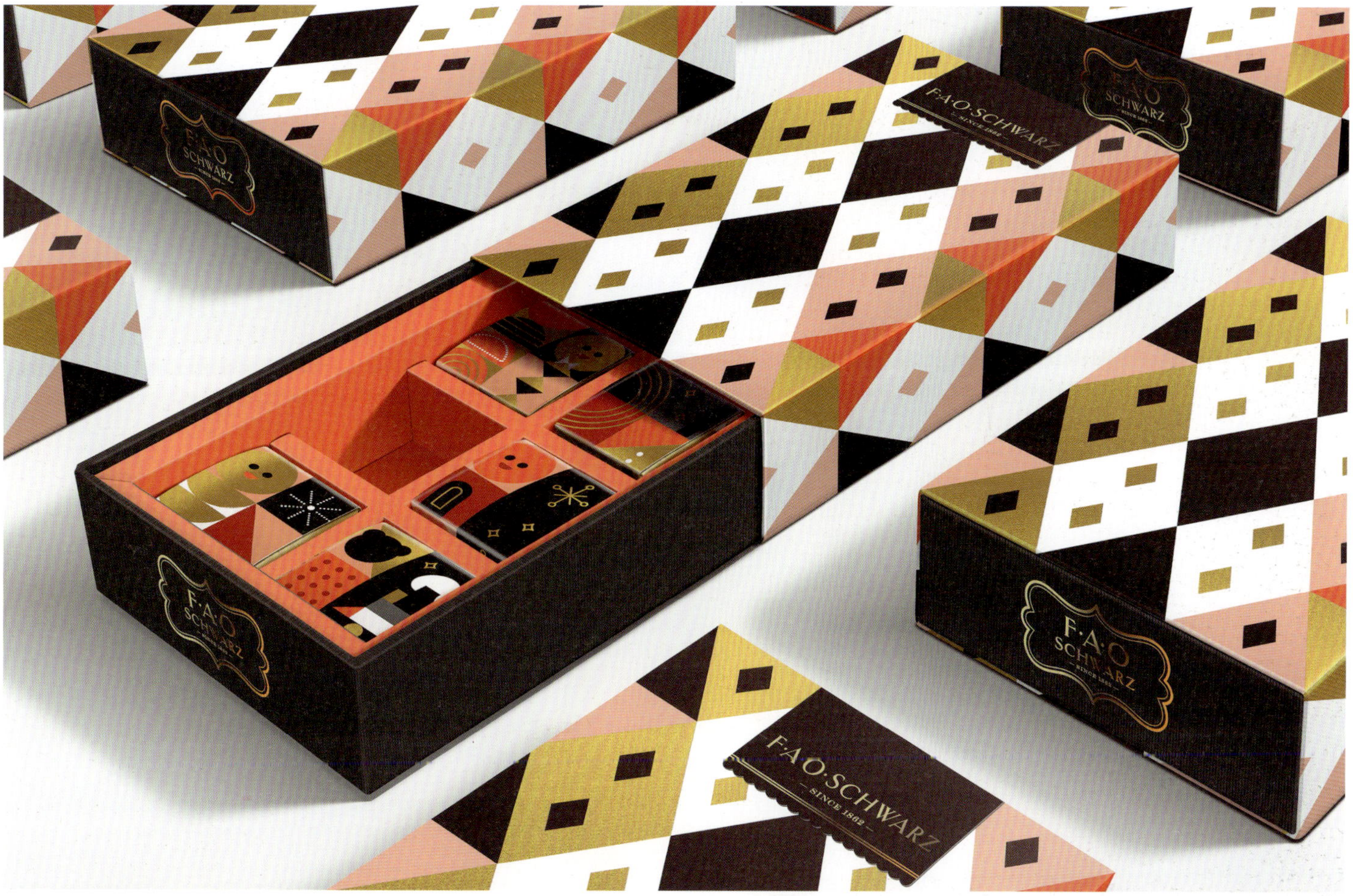

F·A·O·SCHWARZ
SINCE 1862

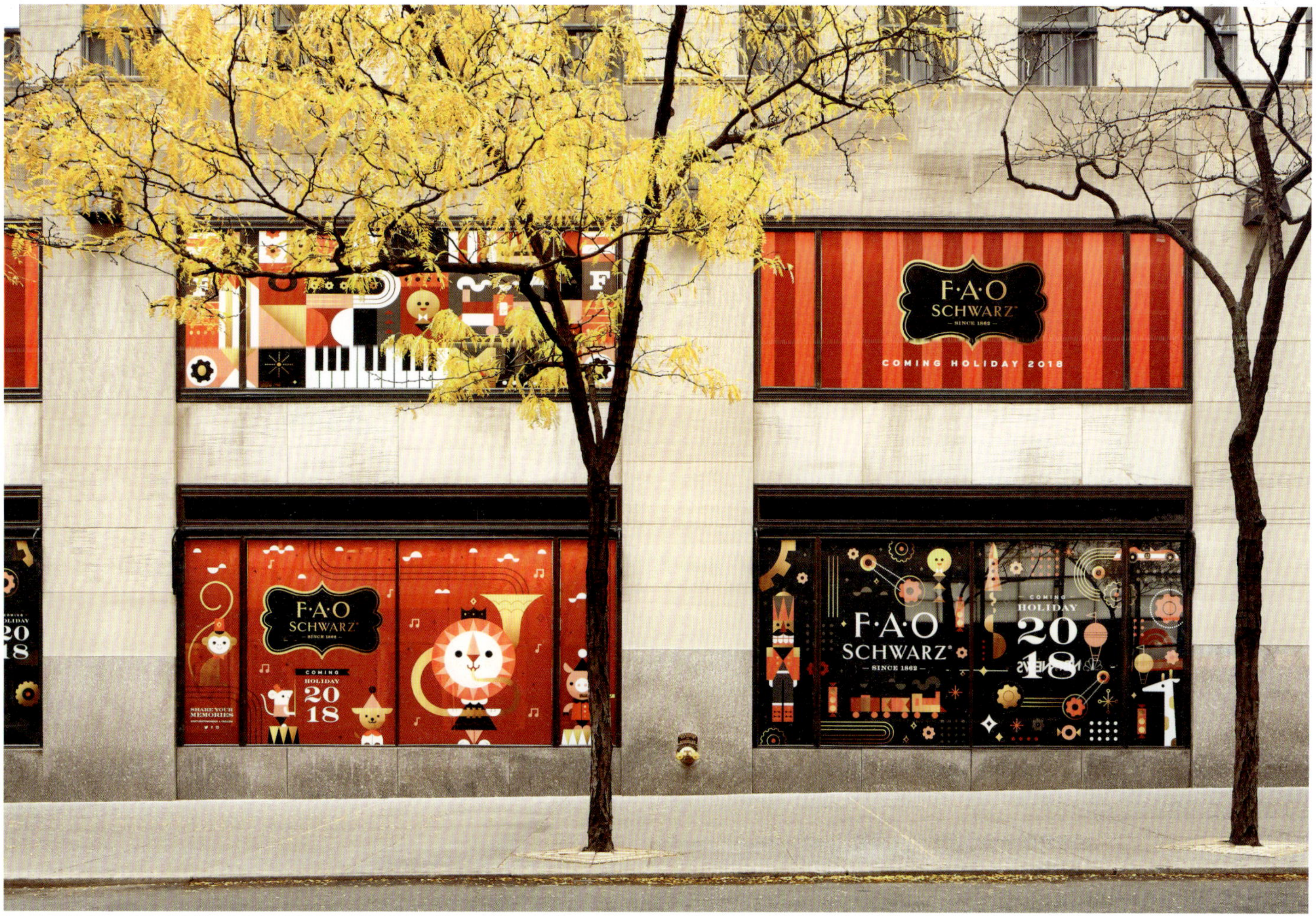

F·A·O
SCHWARZ
SINCE 1862
COMING HOLIDAY 2018

AD
Yuma Harada

DS
UMA/design
farm

2018

POCHI-PON

Cylindrical pouch bag. When you open the lid, you hear a "PON" happy sound.

WATERCOLOR-COLLECTION

D
Nendo

P
Akihiro Yoshida

2018

An eighteen-piece metal furniture collection inspired by the effects of watercolor paint on a paper surface.
To express the idea of paper, the objects are designed to look as though they were cut and folded by hand. In order to create a foundation that resembles paper and to easily blur the ink paint on the objects, the metal frames and surfaces, which are the substrate materials, were repeatedly and thoroughly sanded, applied with primer and finished with matte white paint.
To create beautiful color bleeds as if soaked in the furniture with perfect blurring expressions, all painting was done by hand, section by section, tapping the paint gently with soft pulp paper. This meticulous coloring process was created with a mix of two tones of aqueous inks which takes time to dry, and the objects are finished with a protective clear matte layer that further accentuates their flat paper-like appearance.

SUNNYGOGO

AD, CD & D
Jiayun Liu

DS
LIUJIAYUN Design Studio

P
Shiyue Photographic Studio

2017

SunnyGoGo interprets fruit crispy with art. Cubism pursues forms of fragmentation, resolution and recombination. Artists depict objects in fragmented combinations from multiple angles. The combinations are placed in one same picture to present the most complete image of the object.
This technique is applied to re-elaborate the existing processing procedures of form, destruction, combination and transformation for fruit crispy. The packaging for mango crisp and pineapple crisp is presented in a 4-fluorescent-color fruit polygonal section, complemented by a black fruit realistic illustration. The idea of every craftsman who makes the crispy is presented in an optimum color ratio which brings people sunny feelings with bright and cheerful colors.

sunnygogo
dried fruit

陽光菓菓
sunnygogo
dried fruit

PONYO PORCO QUANTUM SYSTEM
ILLUSTRATION CALENDAR 2019

The concept was an interplanetary observation ship's discovery of a wise quantum beyond the generation in the galaxy. The captain and his crew recorded the fantastic scenes they saw every month.
A dozen of prominent illustrators were invited to work on this calendar. The cover used transparent plastic acrylics accompanied by classic fonts in iron silver. The inside pages adopted illustrations in lively and bright RISO print colors while the back cover used premium silver paper imprinted with screen print white ink, to integrally represent the record of time and space.

AD, CD & D
Larry Chen

A
Larry Chen, Kao Shan, Dashan Bao, 57
Art Studio, ROUND OFF, Shanbi Princess,
Kuangkuang Xu, Shiqi Peng & Yuting
Yang

DS
PONYO PORCO STUDIO

P
Larry Chen

2017

CD & D
Felix Salut

DS
Felix Salut

P
Vytautas Kumza

2018

GALAPAGOS GAME

The Galapagos game takes its name from the Galapagos Islands, home to a vast number of unique species and similar to the countless unique typographic and abstract iterations that can be made with the building blocks.
Based on principles of self-learning, the Galapagos Game teaches the joy of discovery. The original version is very exclusive, with each of the 45 blocks handmade 75 × 75 × 15mm in size.
The pocket version of the game is a portable version with 25 × 25 × 3mm blocks, altogether 54 building blocks printed with nine different geometric shapes that can be laid out to form endless combinations of letters, words or more abstract artistic expressions.
The original incarnation of the game has been acquired by the Stedelijk Museum in Amsterdam for its permanent collection and is set to be a design classic.

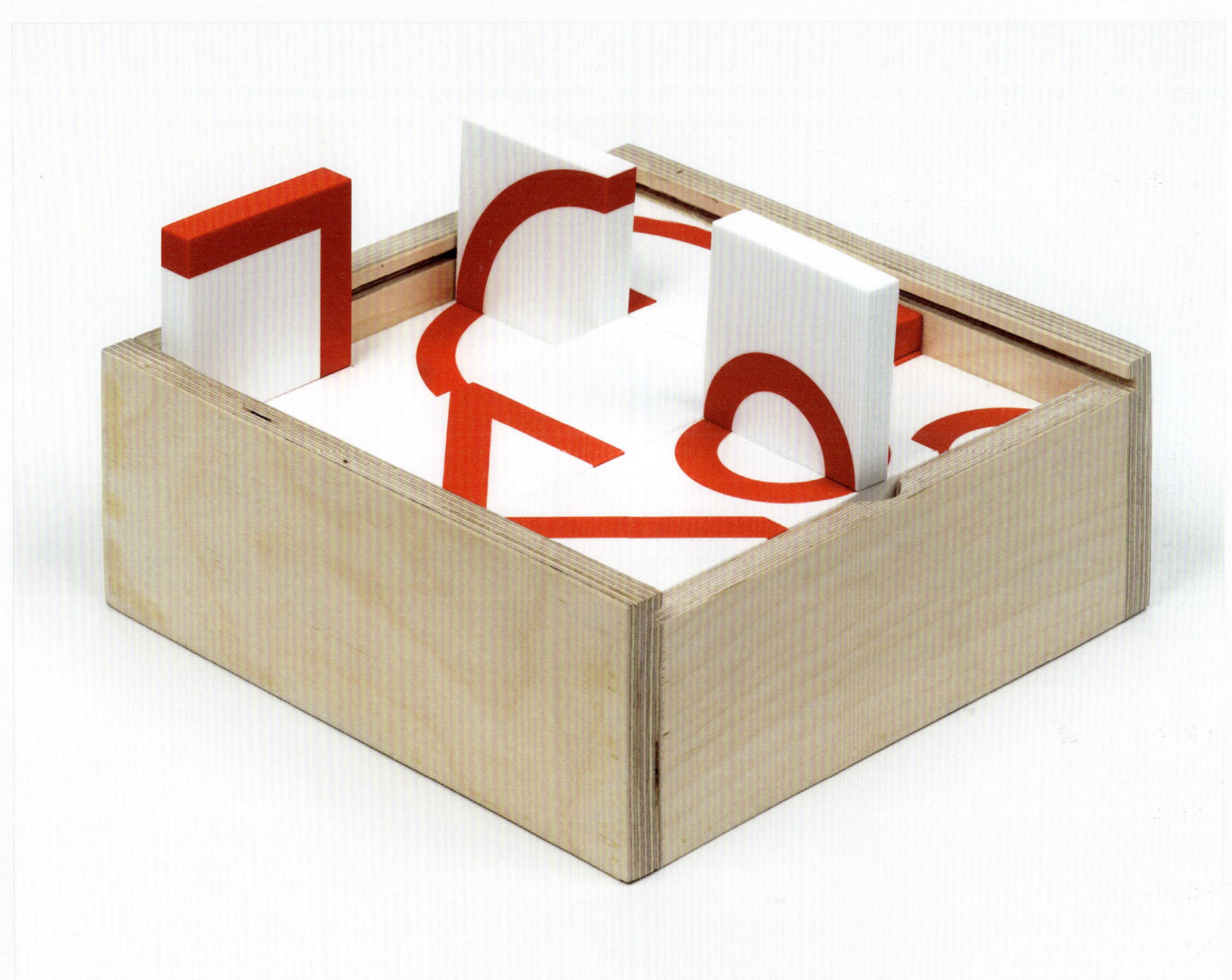

GO RECYCLE

AD
Bryan Satalino

D
Ruoxue Wang

DS
Ruoxue Wang Design

P
Austen Hart

2018

Go Recycle is an eco-friendly educational toy that's suitable for all ages. By playing with it, people learn which materials are supposed to be recycled and which are not. What's fun about this is the process of playing the game imitates the actual physical action of throwing an object into a real trashcan, so it becomes a good practice for real-life recycle.

MOODCAST FRAGRANCE CO.

The gold foiled circle is the central design element intended to communicate one's personal space or atmosphere. The circle is a theme that is executed in a multitude of ways throughout the product experience.
For the glassware the studio designed individually colored matte-glass vessels with a translucent circular window to reinforce the concept of personal space and highlight the flame as it burns. Colors are inspired by the 1960s Finnish glassware & accessories and the principles of colour-therapy to create a palette that helps reinforce each mood.

IN

AD, CD & D
Fredericus L'Ami

DS
Studio L'Ami

P
Fredericus L'Ami

2018

HIDE AND SEEK

D
Yuri Himuro

DS
Himuro Design Studio Inc.

P
Masahiro Muramatsu

2017

This is a collection of playful jacquard textiles with contrasting images on each side, made possible by creatively manipulating the woven mechanism. Under the theme "hide and seek", you will discover a hidden story not shown on the front side of the textile on its backside. For example, the backside of the textile that shows something hiding behind a car is a kitty trying to catch a birdie. This collection takes on hidden living animals such as people and sea creatures doing something else on its backside of the textile.

D
Yuri Himuro

DS
Himuro Design Studio Inc.

P
Kohsuke Higuchi

2018

WHITE CHRISTMAS

You will find some Christmas gifts underneath the white surface. This textile would
be a Christmas tree after you cut the white yarn.

LOVE

MIW'S TAIL A FAIRY TALE

Product concept is a picture book, and the packaging makes it look like a book. It is finished in a soft design, with the worldview of the unique illustrations used.

IN

AD, CD & D
Koji Matsumoto

DS
Grand Deluxe

2016

KOTEN

AD, CD & D
COCHAE

P
Harumi Obama

2007

Original "CHIENO Origami" was published between the 1920s and 1930s. Some of the traditional auspicious motifs: crane, turtle, Fukusuke, frog, and some of Cochae's new
designs: headpiece and cicada, are reprinted. The completed origami can be stored in
the package box. English illustrated instructions are included.

THE ORIGINAL OF THE GRAPHIC ORIGAMI
古典おりがみ
元祖絵付折紙シリーズ第 3 弾！
1921年発行の『チエノ折紙』を大胆にアレンジしたコチャエの定番！
2004年の発行から愛されてきた古典シリーズが堂々リニューアル！
伝承折紙をベースにしているので楽しみながら日本文化を知ることが
できます！
福助 Fukusuke
扇子
おかめ
福助
＊順を追って折ると3段階で図柄が変わります。
鶴 Crane
亀 Turtle
兜 Helmet
蛙 Frog
蝉 Cicada
6 種類　　（135mm×135mm）　各 3 枚／全 18 枚 + 折図付
6 types　（135mm×135mm）　each 3 / all 18 + diagram
※注意　折り紙は食べ物ではありません。誤って
飲み込んだりしないでください。折り上がった作
品で危険な遊びをしないでください。折り紙は薄
いので、指などを切らないように注意してください。
MADE IN JAPAN　design by COCHAE
外装：PP
4 573231 340024

COCHAE
戦前折紙 古典おりがみ
1921に発行された『チエノ折紙』のアレンジ復刻
福助、鶴、亀、蝉、兜、蛙の6種類

HINAYA ORIGAMI AND SHOP CARD

AD, CD & D
COCHAE

P
Harumi Obama

2013

It is the collaboration with Hinaya Kyoto. Fox origami shop card and Hinaya original origamis.

MY FIRST NEEDLEWORK

AD
Mayuko Kato

CD
Yuji Tokuda

D
Mayuko Kato

DS
canaria inc.

2013

The first time for anything is always a time of anxiety. Because of this, there must
be something to stimulate one's imagination and make it fun at the start. So, lay out
the shape to be born from the colors of the threads in the embroidery frame, which is
like a picture frame, and create a little world. The feeling of anticipation toward
the completion is the first excitement that makes it fun.

bienvenue!
petit broderie
はじめてのししゅう

bienvenue!
petit broderie
はじめてのししゅう

ROCKETO

AD, CD & D
Arunas Matacius

DS
ROCKETO

2018

ROCKETO aims to set up new standards for dog product design.
Most of the dog food packaging are overcrowded and outdated. The designer wanted to emphasize how the product can benefit dog's life, but not to highlight content. He wanted design to be simple, yet functional. Carrying a 4kg box might be a challenge for a fragile female dog owner. That is why the designer made dog paw cuts on the sides. Fish might be smelly for luxury apartment that is why he uses zip lock pouches.

ROCKETO
HEMP
IN MCT
FULL SPECTRUM
CO2 EXTRACTED OIL 30ml

ROCKETO
BALTIC SARDINES

COLORFUL DRAWING 2018

SPRING COLLECTION

Products of Colorful Drawing are configured with warm and lyrical watercolored-color like spring. So designers created a package that looks like the watercolor tone of spring. This graphic is inspired by the spring that makes all of life born and be fresh. So they expressed it with bright and soft watercolor.
The mission was to make "Colorful Drawing" look like a product of Etude House (lovely and cute), but lyrical and calm like watercolor. (They looked like contrast concepts.) So designers had many attempts in drawing touch and color using watercolor for mood like Etude House's. It is too hard to draw watercolor images with digital tools, so they tried testing watercolor with hand drawing, scanning it many times, and finally got the result they wanted.

AD
Jang Young Jin (Etude House)

CD
Choi Rita

D
Park Yun Je (ohSeven) & Gu Song-e (ohSeven)

DS
ohSeven

P
Grapher

CL
Etude House

2018

BranDiscovery®

Life

Is

A

Festival

Life Is A Festival

Festivals are usually memorable days in our life. Most of them originated from traditional folklore and religion; some stemmed from commemoration for certain people or events while some are the days on which campaigns advocated by international organizations take place. To celebrate festivals, people normally gather together and have certain activities.

As social economy and culture evolve, modern festivals are no longer restricted to conventional categories and a much wider variety of festivals are born, such as shopping festivals, food festivals, film festivals and music festivals etc. These festivals do not only embody people's attention and love for life, but also depict our keen interest to share things, ideas and emotions in diversely hilarious ways.

Festivals in all ages have always been a social bond to connect people in the spirit of goodwill. The celebrations offer a sense of belonging for religious, social, or geographical groups, contributing to group cohesiveness. On this basis, the colorful modern festivals produce more fun and nutrients for our heart. The increasingly elaborate categories of festivals have been building platforms for people with common interests, allowing them to willfully play, chat, share, explore and enjoy the wonders life has to offer!

01.
Water Arts

AD & CD & D
Iara Grinspun

2017

FILTRO

This is a water-arts festival, which involves a wide variety of disciplines, such as cinematography, music, sports, painting, etc. The proposal of the project is to immerse into the fantastic universe of water. Make sure that being under water brings us another dimension.
The main concept aims to create a parallelism between arts and the swimming world. That's why it is shown with perspective typographies, and surreal illustrations that passes through different elements. This festival has the power to make the fluency of water alive. So the idea is to go through the filter. Jump, dive and swim.

FESTIVAL
DE ARTES ACUÁTICAS
Filtro
FESTIVAL
Ne plongez pas dans le petit bain
BRASSE
PLANCHES

02.
Arts

AD & CD
Chang Pu-Hui

D
Chang Pu-Hui

DS
changph.com

2018

TAIPEI ARTS
FESTIVAL 2018

Visuals for the 2018 Taipei Arts Festival themed Assembly. Since there were only three sites for displaying posters, it was difficult to propagandize the activity. So the visual carrier was changed into tote bags which were given out in large quantities and became live advertisements moving around in the city. The main visual exchanged characteristics of ordinary things to distinguish themselves and attract people's eyes. Also, plenty of big bright color blocks were printed on the bags to make people who carried them spotlights in a crowd and more like participants of the festivals. Moreover, the tote bags could make up a poster visual when patched. The festival includes a lot of open-air performances without space for written guide. Filled in with heavy stuffs and piled up a bit, the bags could make a standing plate and visual wall to guide the participants while echoing the theme at the same time.

FESTIVAL
TAIPEI ARTS
8.8-10.21
20.
ANNIV.
臺
藝1
臺北
藝術節。
"ASSEMBLY" 為了___在一起。

03.
Film

AD
Maude Bussières

2018

REEL HEART FILM
FESTIVAL - THE DIRECTOR'S CUT

This is the unselected work for Reel Heart Toronto International Film Festival. This platform is composed of two types of visuals: a visual to create awareness by only using the name of the festival and the other is the imagery to promote the spirit of the festival. These two types of posters are meant to live together. The imagery is inspired by the emotions that submerge a human being while watching a movie.

Reel Heart
FILM FESTIVAL
JULY 03—08
REELHEART.COM

Reel Heart
FILM FESTIVAL
REEL HEART
JULY 03—08
REELHEART.COM

Reel Heart
FILM FESTIVAL
JULY 03—08
REELHEART.COM

Reel Heart
FILM FESTIVAL
JULY 03—08
REELHEART.COM

AD
Begad Hassan

CD
Khalil El shorbagy

D
Khalil El Shorbagy &
Begad Hassan

DS
JWT (Cairo)

2016

38th CAIRO
INTERNATIONAL FILM FESTIVAL

38th Cairo International Film Festival and branding. Taking a new approach to festival identities that were perceived as old bak, designers wanted to create something different that year, something that can compete with foreign film festivals.

D
Gustavo Estevão

DS
Gustavo Estevão Design

P
Aline Gabriel & Diego Neves

2016

INTERSESSÕES—
FILM FESTIVAL

Intersessões is a film festival that takes place in Ubá, an interior city in Brazil. To engage its targets, the name was created by combining the words "Interior" and "Session" of a movie. The brand used plenty of different Cartesian planes in intersections, intending to symbolize the encounter of the most varied types of people, having the cinema as its agent.
Beyond the planes, the logotype is composed by a photograph with different weights for each letter, making reference to the old roll films used by the movie theaters.
The identity also counts with graphic elements inspired by surrealism art. Among the utilized images, Ary Barroso, an important figure in Brazilian national culture scene, stands out.

04.
Music

AD, CD & D
**Maxime Pirot &
Alice Bouchardon**

DS
Studio OUAM

2018

TRÈS COOL
MUSIC FESTIVAL

Studio OUAM created a new branding for the first edition of Très Cool, a music festival. It takes place in the countryside of France, Deauville, a city well known for its beaches and iconic stripes of its sunshades, but with meadows, apple and pear orchards too. Designers decided to show this other face of the city, by mixing the stripes of the beach with the French countryside symbols, to have a very fun and playful identi-ty. Two types are contrasting: the bold and friendly Cooper with the very chic and elegant Roxborough. They used a fun color palette and created many small illustrations to have a lot of elements to play with on each communication support!

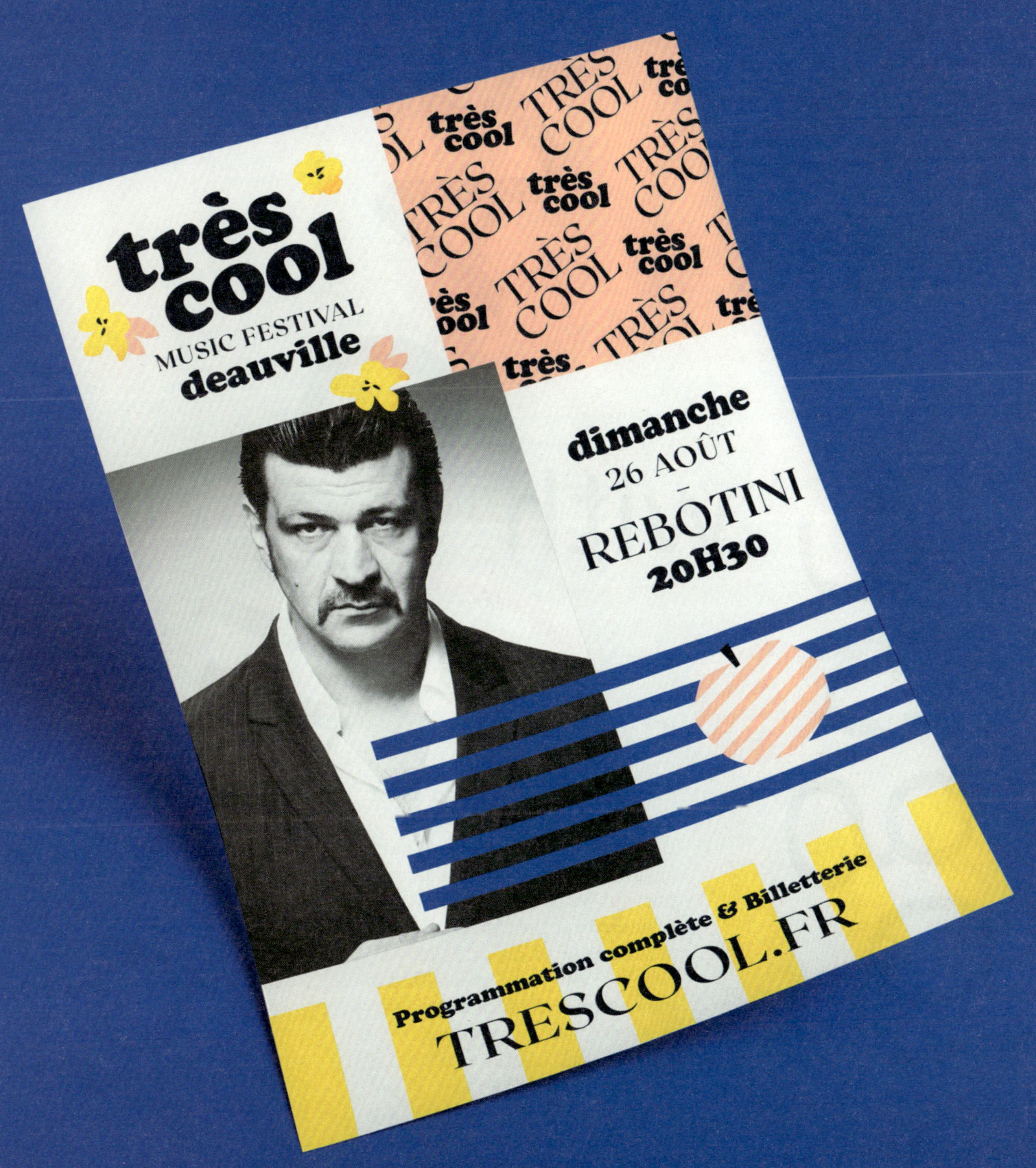

très cool
MUSIC FESTIVAL
deauville
TRÈS COOL
très cool
dimanche
26 AOÛT
–
REBOTINI
20H30
Programmation complète & Billetterie
TRESCOOL.FR

Dialogue with IARA GRINSPUN

Iara Grinspun

Graphic designer and art director based in Buenos Aires, Argentina. Her work is fun, clear and dynamic. Always seeking for visual impact but without losing clarity. A graduate at the Universidad of Buenos Aires, majoring in Graphic Design and specialized in Illustration and Editorial Design, Grinspun has been working in agencies as DHNN, MediaMonks, and Possible Worldwide. As a designer, she's always trying to bring new ways of communicating into this world. For her, it is essential to materialize the concepts and then finally give them an identity. Make them real.

Interviewer
Virginia Ruan

It's always positive to exchange information and knowledge sometimes.

Can you give some more introduction on the arts-festival Filtro?
Filtro festival was created as a University project in which I was encouraged to design the main concept of the brand and its graphic elements, including the name.
It's a 3-day festival from 9:00 to 23:00. There are activities during the day such as photography expositions, contemporary arts exhibitions and synchronized swimming competitions. Light & Water shows are provided during the night, as you can also find film projections and live music bands.
The festival branding includes 42 different graphic items, such as a printed brochure, banner, flyer, web, app, tote-bag, ticket, towel, and others.

How did you come out with the main concept for this visual? What effects do you want to create or what feelings would you like to evoke with this design?
I wanted to merge the water world and the arts, so I thought about a common word to name the festival, such as "Filtro" which in Spanish means "filter". Filter is used in the cinematographic industry and also to "filter water". So the aimed concept is to pass through the filter and discover the new perspectives that water can bring us. Jump, dive and swim! According to this, I've used isometric elements to graphic the concept and some illustrations that pass through other illustrations as well.

Do you yourself like water arts? Which do you like best or are you good at?
I like water arts because it comes from a natural state, and it is mostly represented through organic shapes. But I am afraid I am not good at them.

What kind of festivals do you like? And what do you think of participation in festival activities?
I am really a fan of music festivals, I know its cliché, but let's face it, they are amazing. I also like editorial/ book fairs in which you can meet authors and learn from them.
Participating in any festival activities is super interesting in order to meet people from other disciplines, countries and cultures. It's always positive to exchange information and knowledge sometimes.

What are the popular festivals in Argentina? Can you name some and tell us about them?
In Argentina music and film festivals are the most popular ones, electronic music parties are the BOMB. Of course we have food festivals which rocks, but they are not as popular as the music ones.
Some of the festivals I most like here in Argentina are: Lollapaloza (music), Masticar (food), BAF (fashion), BAFICI (film).

Life Is A Festival.

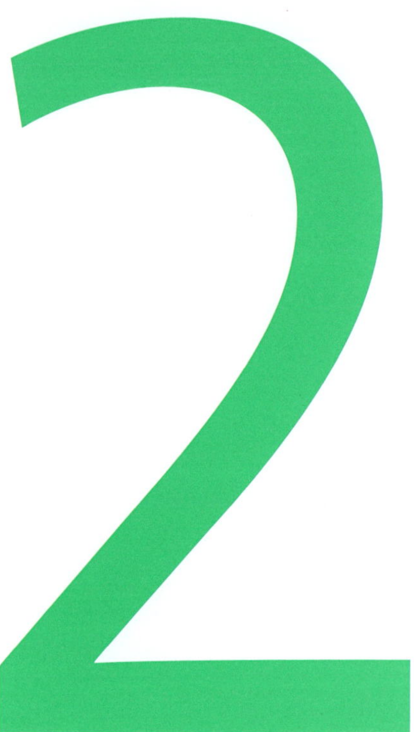

out

When outdoors, we hope to always stay radiant. Hence, the things we bring with us can hardly be overemphasized. Take along cosmetics with damsel temperaments, childlike and chic brooches, cute Furoshikis and handkerchiefs, a vitamin and supplement pack combining DJ turntable into the look, an album recording the singers' emotions, and have a lick of a colorfully flavored ice cream, or sip a cup of coffee cuddling with an adorable pet. This, would definitely make a perfect outdoor experience.

So let's see how designers add stunning beauty to our life with their fantasy and exquisite crafts!

Dialogue with JOE FANG

Joe Fang

Designs should be alive. They live in the stories of the people we design for. A design only lives when there is a person involved. We always listen before we create, so that our designs come from solid memories and form warm reminders to those we design for: never forget what's most precious to you.

Music is no doubt a great and wonderful achievement in human cultural history. An art form integrating sound, sense of hearing, emotions and time, music reflects human's real life and sentiments. Restraining, gushing, ethereal and elegant, or smoothing, music allows everyone to open and freely float in any way he likes. Everyone can be sad, joyful, irresolute, depressive or confused without any preparedness and camouflage.The flow of music has the magic to set free all of our emotions, and envelop us with the safest protection screen it instantly creates. Awakening the heart's resonance vibrations and soothing the soul - such is its power to allure.

Albums have been the physical carrier for music. And the design of albums reveals the core of the music it carries. A good design is undoubtedly a formfitting suit to highlight the music's figure and romantic charm, thus tempting its audience. Joe Fang, Taiwan's album design master, is always able to seize the traits of singers and musicians, distill the essence of the music and add brilliance to its existing splendor. Dreaming to enter the movie circle since his childhood, Joe as a designer has long developed a style of plotting every piece of work into a story. It is exactly the souled designs he created that have been nominated as the "Best Album Packaging" for the Golden Melody Awards for a dozen times and even bagged the Golden Pin Design Award. Nevertheless, having designed about 100 albums, Joe hopes his works go without any style. All the while, he deems album design shall serve the music and enable the latter to be "seen". Music relates to the sense of hearing, but if it can be seen, it means design has added to its wonder. Such is a "right" design for Joe.

He likes to immense in music and interact with the audience. He listens to every song, tries to comprehend the lyrics, figures out the audience's temperaments and the heat the music attempts to transfer, feels the temperature he really receives, and finally accommodates it into the album. This is the design which he thinks will indeed trigger imagination.

Editor
Virginia Ruan

Music to Be "Seen"

Interviewer

Virginia Ruan

Only when a design is done on the basis of affirmed demands in a suggestive way is it a right design.

You said in a previous interview that "It is easy to make a good-looking design, but difficult to make a right one". So what a right design is like in your eyes?
A designer's task is to solve problems rather than make packages for others with absolute aesthetics. Therefore, only when a design is done on the basis of affirmed demand and specific problems to tackle in a suggestive way is it a right design. Of course, aesthetic perception shall be considered.

Your works are nominated as the "Best Album Packaging" for the Golden Melody Awards for a dozen times. How did you get exposed to album design at the very beginning?
Before I was enrolled in the military, I worked at Rose Music and have been exposed to visuals and music ever since. A strong interest in music was therefore cultivat-ed and I became increasingly curious about ways to connect visuals with music. Later on I got opportuni-ties to work on design and began to regard visuals as a way to communicate with music. That is why I hope to continuously make album jackets with "visualized music".

You have been involved in album design for years and have dealt with various kinds of music. What kind of music do you like? Is there any singer whom you would like to cooperate with?
I like different music in different phases. Actually music has long blended in my life and work. So I try as many types of music as possible, to find more music that fits myself. I would like to work with Chinese singers like Cheer Chen and Eason Chan, since I very much like their music but haven't got any chance to collaborate with

them. I would also like to cooperate with overseas singers or musicians, to further explore the link between abstract visual presentation and music. Besides this, I hope I am courageous enough to face future challenges.

How many members do you have now in your team? How do you communicate or get along with your team?
We have seven staff now, and we may work with other people in accordance with the scale or nature of cases. We often discuss with each other. When I make a design, I would ask them to have a look at it and give me suggestions. And my colleagues would also ask for advice on their works. We want to challenge ourselves, overthrow our thoughts and discuss more in limited time, to invest considerations from multiple angles into our works.

You and your team designed the posters, videos and the motion design on stage for the 54th and 55th Golden Horse Awards. Motion design is more widely spread than static graphic design. So what is the challenge for you in this sphere?
It is a great challenge to turn graphic design three-dimensional and then a story. But only with challenges can I make myself stronger and absorb energies from more fields to push me forward.

You love drawing and storytelling since childhood and dream of entering the movie circle. And you have been emphasizing imagery in your design, using your skillful pen to draw the fantasy in your heart for albums and stage plays. Can we say that it has realized your dream of entering the movie circle to some extent?
Actually I did not expect to touch the movie field, my most desirable field, in such a short time. It's just that I have the opportunity to tap it with design, so I try my best to do it. But I think my dream has not yet come truc. Now it is just the beginning. I hope to grow capable enough to really participate in a movie.

You have a pet cat named Hao Ba whom you like to often post on your Instagram page. What's his temperament like? Is he clingy? How do you get along with him?
Hao Ba is quite good-tempered and just hisses when he's angry. He's really nice to everyone so he becomes even a PR cat. Whether you come to the office for the first time or not, he would probably jump onto your thighs. I often go out for meetings, but as long as I stay at the office, he would sit by my keyboard and stare at me very close. He likes to walk and walk on our worktables. During the breaks, I would stay with him on the couch in the living room.

ALBUM OF MAYDAY-HISTORY
OF TOMORROW (USB VERSION)

AD & CD
Joe Fang

D
Joe Fang & Hitsu Pi

DS
JOEFANGSTUDIO

P
Hideaki Hamada,
Toyokazu Nagano
& Jingping Yu

2016

The main concept was memoir, so the style was decided as classic but simple and pure. Photos are tranquil sceneries in daily life, scenes familiar to the band. Allow Mayday to take their fans back to where the dream started off. The album gathered design energies from different regions: photographers from Japan, font designers from Hong Kong and a design team from Taiwan. Moreover, the designers hid the USB stick in the cassette, to get back to the initial modality of music with the change of media. It was also meant for paying tribute to the purest age. Of course, the design of the USB stick did not restrain to the function of information carrier; it could also be a necklace which could catch up with the pace of modern society and allowed fans to be always with Mayday.

AD & CD
Joe Fang

D
Joe Fang & Hitsu Pi

DS
JOEFANGSTUDIO

P
Tingkuei Shao

2018

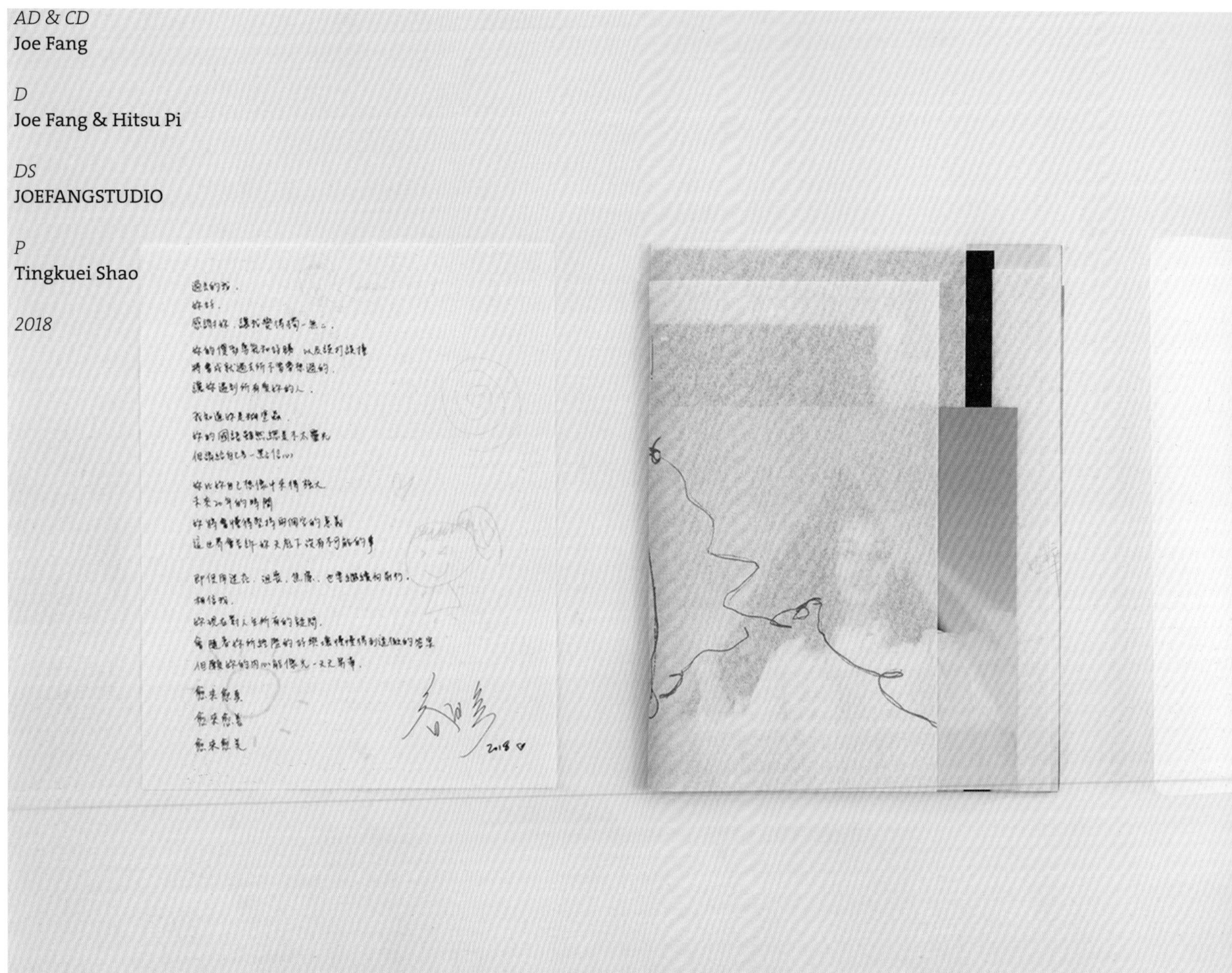

JOEY YUNG-SEARCHING FOR ANSWERS

In this album, the singer Joey Yung would like to share with the audiences her accumulated life experience and self-analysis on the way searching for her own "answer" over the years. So the design was based on a stage play with black-and-white plane photography as the main line, supplemented by the mood records and sketchings from Joey. In this album imbued with her moods and traces, paper of varied permeability and textures is used to stack, to symbolize the accumulation since she made her debut.

HUSH-TO SAY IT IN ANOTHER WORD

AD & CD
Joe Fang

D
Joe Fang & FKWU

DS
JOEFANGSTUDIO

P
Manbo Key, ChienWen Lin & MW
studio TW

2018

To represent the concept of "To Say It in Another Word" and echo the last song of this album "Sleepwalk", designers inlayed the dreamy gorgeousness to the pure white and clean album image in a high contrast way. So they used imported invisible ink to express the images in multiple orientations.
In ordinary light, nothing appears special. Only in the light of the UV flashlight attached with the album, can the pictures and lyrics hidden be seen. The effects are even better without light. Fans can feel the two different appearances by turning the lights on and off to sleepwalk with HUSH.

AMUYI-O_LOVE

AD & CD
Joe Fang

D
Joe Fang, FKWU & East Lin

DS
JOEFANGSTUDIO

P
Chung Lun Wu

2017

With the album name "O_LOVE", designers conceived of on the singer Amuyi's favorite things to shared all the "LOVE" in her life with her fans. The main line of the story setting is to personalize her favorite pet as a good company in her way to music. In order to build a world for Amuyi, designers worked with artistic designers to set up animated scenes with scene installations and then took the pictures in the studio. The cover image was taken from an angle similar to that of the personalized pet, so as to create the fun of double covers.

AMUYI
O_LOV
O_LOV
O_LO

09 How come
怎麼會

MEN ENVY CHILDREN-ONE THING

AD & CD
Joe Fang

D
Joe Fang & FKWU

DS
JOEFANGSTUDIO

P
Evan Huang & Lie Chen

2016

"One Thing" symbolizes the one thing that the band has been endeavouring to do. The designers adopted machine embroidery, aggregating different colored lines to form letters, characters and doodles, to make the entire look more dynamic and childlike. It can not only express the band's perseverance in chasing their dream on the road to music, but also echo the theme of this album, One Thing. Liveliness, purity, simpleness and accumulation is what the band and designers want to pass on to the fans.

06　妳，這個小東西

YOU,
MY LITTLE THING

Dialogue with HELEN DOWNIE

Helen Downie

Working under the moniker of Unskilled Worker, the London-based, self-taught artist rose to prominence via her hugely successful Instagram account. Drawing upon a broad spectrum of influences, her evocative work has an intimate quality that draws the viewer into a highly atmospheric world of childlike innocence, suggestive of darker times.

Illustration, a major form of art, has always been the sector attracting most attention in the art world. "Fashion", is something that has an ever-changing definition in different time periods. When fashion encounters illustration, they enlighten brilliant and breath-taking sparkles. We can say that fashion and illustration have been pairing in the past century. Books with costume graphics first appeared in the 16th to 17th century. In the end of the 17th century, the collecting of these costume graphics became popular and "fashion" as a topic appeared in magazines for the first time. Then in the 18th century, pocket books with miniature black and white fashion illustrations grew to be a great success. And the two sectors finally blended to appear in magazines in the end of the 18th century.

In this current age, fashion brands are also keeping their close ties with illustrations, which boosts the brand's artistic image on the one hand, and diverts more attention to the illustrations full of fun on the other. The popular platform of Instagram even allows many to make a figure and become popular among people.

Well known for her colorful figures with wide-set eyes, London-based artist Helen Downie discovered painting at 48—and, without any formal training, rose to international fame in under two years. Her cooperation with fashion mammoth Gucci gains her considerable fame and makes a very popular fashion illustrator in the recent two years. *The New York Times* says Helen is "A Late-Bloomer Artist Finds Instagram - and Fashion" while *The Times*

Editor
Virginia Ruan

A Long-forgotten Dream

defines her as "The British housewife who became the darling of Gucci". After a battle with cancer and a detox from alcohol and drugs, this British housewife with 4 children picked up the painting brush in 2013 almost by accident, sketching with a friend. Calling herself an "unskilled worker", Helen ushers in the dawn of her life and becomes a darling of the fashion industry in her fifties, with her true passion towards painting and exceptional observation. For her, painting is a long-forgotten dream and now she has a lifetime of material to draw upon.

Helen says she has always been fascinated by the way people invent themselves through appearance. It is a creative choice everybody has to make. So when she started painting, it was only natural that this would become part of her work. Her paintings are built around these characters, how they wear their clothes and what they wish to project or hide. That is what she is fascinated with: what people use. She has always enjoyed fashion as a way of creating herself. Fashion is important, because it affects people in themselves. How we dress mostly reflects what we wish to reflect. She thinks fashion helps us to be a better version of ourselves. On another level, fashion teaches us about history and culture and can challenge boundaries in much the same way as art. They have always found each other irresistible.

It is the eyes, big and beautiful, that we first notice when we look at Helen's portraits. They are like the eyes of her own, wide-set and curvaceous like a cat's, blue like the sky. What are the stories behind these intriguing eyes? Let's listen to the talk.

Interviewer
Virginia Ruan

I think I am always trying to get back to my childhood; to get back to the wonder I felt as a seven-year-old and to take people with me.

SOAVE AMORE
LOVE

All I really want to do is paint.

Why do you use the pseudonym Unskilled Worker to name your Instagram account and your personal website? I am really curious about it.

I had the name in my head for a long time, but I didn't know where to put, what to do with it or what it was for. I'm self-taught and so when I started to paint it seemed like the most appropriate name... it still is. I relate to the word.

Your illustrations feature fashionable girls with wide-set and curvaceous eyes, childish but startling. Why do you prefer this style? Are you actually drawing yourself or what life has cast upon you?

I've never really thought about my work in terms of a style; I still don't. My practice of portrait painting has recently evolved to a more narrative style, for the most part in response to a misjustice or a social prejudice. Words trip me up. I find painting clearer and more absolute. I think I am always trying to get back to my childhood; to get back to the wonder I felt as a seven-year-old and to take people with me. I hope to make work that's transportive, I want to feel the way I did as a child looking at my first book. It's very instinctive; it has to feel very comfortable for me to leave a color. I think people can sense in my work that although the line and the color is maybe naive - the emotion in the painting is more suggestive of a past.

How did you begin the collaboration with Gucci? How has it impacted your art practice and life?

The collaboration with Gucci was very organic. One of my paintings was purchased by Gucci and presented to Alessandro Michele as a gift and then I was introduced to him and this wonderful creative conversation began. Then came the offer to exhibit at Shanghai's Minsheng Art Museum. My story feels very separate from my paintings. The story feels like it's happening to someone else and I'm on the outside watching in. I've always felt very humbled that people are interested in what I do. It's been an incredible adventure and at times a little overwhelming. I don't think I've changed but how I live has. Painting everyday means I spend a lot of time by myself. It has a way of teaching me who I am; the things about my character that have caused problems in my life are the same things that drive me to paint.

You discovered painting at 48 and, without any formal training, rose to international fame in less than two years. You said you have always loved fashion, but you have never seen yourself as a fashion illustrator. So what's the prospects or plans for your future creations?

I don't plan too far ahead. I've got a couple of projects which I'm working on but unfortunately I can't discuss. All I really want to do is paint.

Dialogue with NIMURA DAISUKE

Nimura Daisuke

Born in Osaka in 1978, Nimura Daisuke now lives in Tokyo. Since his graduation from art school, Nimura Daisuke has been engaged in work as a freelance illustrator. In 2012, he began his full-time illustration work. In 2014, he moved to Tokyo to work.

Good at the use of rough outlines and simple colors, his illustrations are never disappointing in depicting ordinary people's looks and features. Meanwhile, Daisuke makes illustrations for advertisements, books, TV programs and websites.

During the promotion season in N<u>U</u> Chayamachi District of Osaka, Japan, various illustration posters are posted with scantily-clad girls dancing and yelling, or girls wearing cool sunglasses on which only the words of "Price Down" can be seen. Compared with those jammed promotional copywriting, this kind of illustrating ads are more likely to win people's favor. And these creative works are mostly from Japan's popular illustrator Nimura Daisuke.

With rapid growth in the young generation's spending power, consuming brands are striving to exploit the consumption potential of this group. Illustration, full of appeal, is a medium which spans linguistic boundaries. Daisuke's two-dimensional tender but funny illustrations endow a strong yet non-distracting personal style. Their fine-tuned expression closes the distance between brands and the young generation, thus winning their hearts. Apart from works for commercial ads, books and magazines, Daisuke also draws plenty of diverting works. Most of the characters in his illustrations are small potatoes in life like little cute boys and girls. His works remind us of the familiar and interesting scenes in our own life, the things we have been wanting to do but dare not, or that we had a similar complex, such as funny nonsenses like students eager to throw away all the school books, amusements between young lovers and girls lifting their skirts for teasing. Such childhood secrets are plainly visible in Daisuke's works.

Daisuke's illustrations exactly reflect his attitudes toward life. He always retains vital enthusiasm and humor in the numbing daily life, to follow his own slow pace and record amusing moments with bold lines and simple colors. The little stories which seem eccentric and facetious belong to our collective memory, alluring us to recall what we were like when we initially arrived in this world, with all the most beautiful innocence around.

Editor
Catherin Huang

Intimate Diary

Interviewer
Virginia Ruan

I hope to be able to create illustrations which will bring forth intimacy to people.

Your personal works mostly depict relaxing and fun fragments of daily life. Do you get the aspiration from your own life? Can you share your daily life with us?
My daily life is nothing special. Besides ferrying my daughter to and from school, I work or stay at home doing the housework. I always like recording the satisfying or interesting moments in my diary, adding in music or filming elements to make them into music or cartoons.

The characters in your works are mainly boys and girls who behave nonsensically. Why do you favor characterizing this young group? What features do you think they have?
I think it is because the young group are more fun. This is my personal opinion. For example, when seeing a person dancing a strange dance, a child would smile and say: "He seems to be in a pretty good mood!" But an adult man may mock the dancer thinking "is he insane".

Your current illustrations feature simplicity. Compared with your earlier works, they are quite different in palette and character creation. When did you have the consciousness to shape your art style?
Probably 5 years ago, I think. If I baldly depict the erotic theme, people would think I am a wolf. But if I depict it briefly, people would find my works interesting. Since then, it's been a great fun for me to portray the antics of ordinary people. And the use of the No. 7 fine bamboo pen until now has a great influence on my creation style change.

In the new year greeting cards you made, you recorded the significant moments in your life, from having a love affair to getting married. How have your family and daughter impacted your creation?
Ever since my daughter's birth, the idea to draw diverting images has been growing stronger. I don't want to draw pictures that my wife and daughter think weird or fescennine. Moreover, I refer to my daughter's everyday actions in my creation; her innocent behaviors are the source of my inspiration.

Are you interested in extending your art practice to fields other than magazines, books and advertisements, like designing products?
Actually not long ago, I reconsidered the comic strip *Peanuts* created by Charles Schultz. I thought it would be so great if I could create a work like *Peanuts* one day! It is a work which needs no company of flattering. Although my techniques and experience are far from enough now, I hope to be able to create illustrations which will bring forth intimacy to people.

Ill
Nimura Daisuke

CL
U.I.J Hotel & Hostel

2018

U.I.J X NIMURA DAISUKE PROJECT

U.I.J Hotel & Hostel invited Nimura Daisuke to create two lovely characters "Hotel Girl" and "Hostel Boy" with his unique sense of humor. As one of the opening events, U.I.J released the limited edition of "HOTEL GIRL Reading Pillow" and "HOSTEL BOY Books Tote" as special gifts for their guests. The project delivers the message of U.I.J's spirit successfully: "Reading and traveling are both important ways to explore the world and oneself."

Books don't just go with you,
they take you where you've never been.

U.I.J
HOTEL & HOSTEL
× Nimura
daisuke

AD
Koji Sasaki

CD
Censure Urushizaki

D
Makoto Yamaguchi

Ill
Nimura Daisuke

2018

NU CHAYAMACHI SUMMER BARGAIN 2018

The illustration in NU Chayamachi's sale ad has been in use for three years. Varied from regular print ads, the 3rd version of this ad was promoted through the internet and digital cinema. To fulfill the demand of animation, Nimura designed an image featuring a free dancing girl. Taking this image as the main visual, the ad fascinated customers so much that they just overlooked the "sale" label on the skirt and paid for it.

NU
chayamachi
NU 茶屋町 BARGAIN
7.4 WED – 7.16 MON
SALE

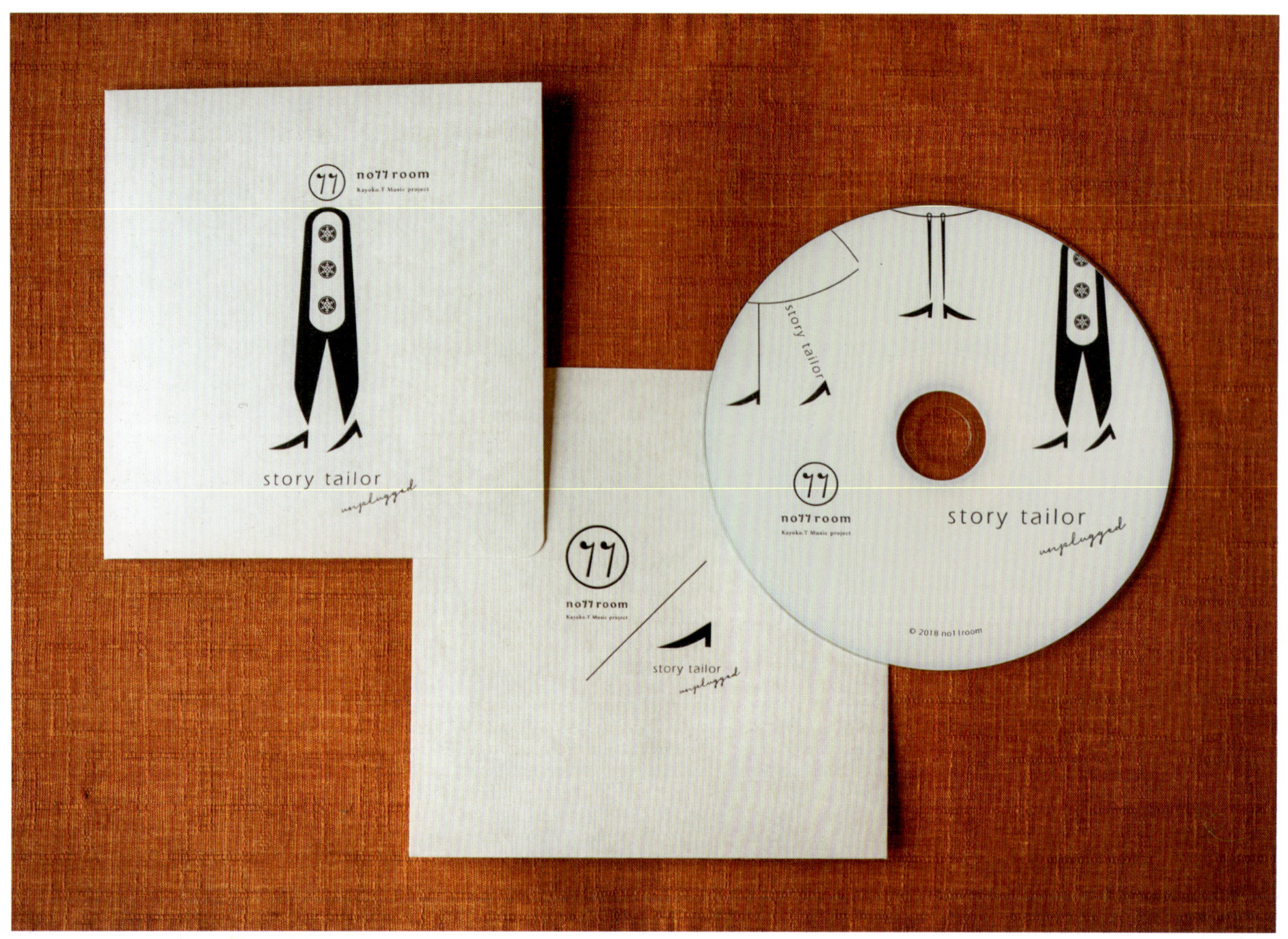

STORY TAILOR

AD, CD & D
Yoshie Tokudome

P
Yoshie Tokudome

2018

A new music album was created for no11rooom, a music artist. The CD packaging is totally made of paper by using A4 envelopes. The entire music album is made up of 6 items such as CD case, case cover, lyric sheet cover, free paper, jacket band, download card and bookmark. This album jacket design is a music album title; the unique logo was created with "Story Tailor" and Japanese katakana notation in mind. Also, opening the inside of the jacket will enter the illustration of the sewing set which has a deep meaning of "weaving the story".

no11 room
Kayoko.T Music project
story tailor

no11 room
Kayoko.T Music project
story tailor

no11 room
Kayoko.T Music project
New Released
ストーリーテラー
01.幻想曲
02.淡く
03.LastDance
04.月の墓で
05.LookAround
06.Film
07.ストーリーは続く
08.忽却の手招き
Sound https://soundcloud.com/no11room
HP http://no11room.tumblr.com

no11 room
Kayoko.T Music project

no77room
Kayoko ~ Music project
story tailor
no77room
Kayoko ~ Music project
Café Bonito
CB-021
¥2000+税
story tailor
Café Bonito CB-021 STEREO
©2018 Café Bonito. All rights Reserved.
no77room
Kayoko ~ Music project
Storytailor

AD & CD
Kurt Glänzer & Josef Heigl

DS
Bruch—Idee&Form

2017

EISPERLE

Ice cream melting in the sun. Various tastes flow into each other while new and fascinating shapes and color combinations are created. With this feeling in mind, designers set out to create the new corporate design concept for the first pure vegan ice cream shop in Graz called "Die Eisperle". The versatile form and color combinations vary on every touch point and communicate a "summerly" attitude to life while showing the creative and adventurous approach of Die Eisperle's curious ice cream varieties. The signet shows the personal ice cream moment and can be adapted to any personality type — because ice cream is something for everyone.

CARD HOLDER

AD
Yuma Harada

DS
UMA/design farm

2018

A lightweight and durable card holder made of wash-resistant paper, also used in cleaning tags with two easy-to-open pockets. Sub-item in wallet or business card case.

DOUBUTSU

AD & D
COCHAE

CD
Toshiko Ohashi & Kensuke Kawamura

2008

Tie the fun, spread the fun, wrap in fun, and fun to look. Depending on the wrapping style, different looks of four "cats" or "dogs" will pop up.
Make a knot with corners of the furoshiki to create the ears, tail or collar, and enjoy the change even in the same face. It can also be a gift wrapping. Wrapping for lunch boxes to make a little bag. Let's try to go out with a favorite dog together.

BURASAGARI FUROSHIKI

AD & D
COCHAE

CD
Toshiko Ohashi & Kensuke Kawamura

2008

With this single wrapping cloth you can make a "hanging animal figure". When you tie in a bag style you will see a variety of unique and charming animals, which is unique and slightly funny with dark humor.

D
Yuri Himuro

DS
Himuro Design Studio Inc.

P
Kazuya Shioi

2010

ONIGIRI HANDKERCHIEF

This is a handkerchief that looks like an Onigiri (Japanese traditional food) when folded into a triangle. When you open it, you can find a symmetrical graphic pattern split by seaweed.

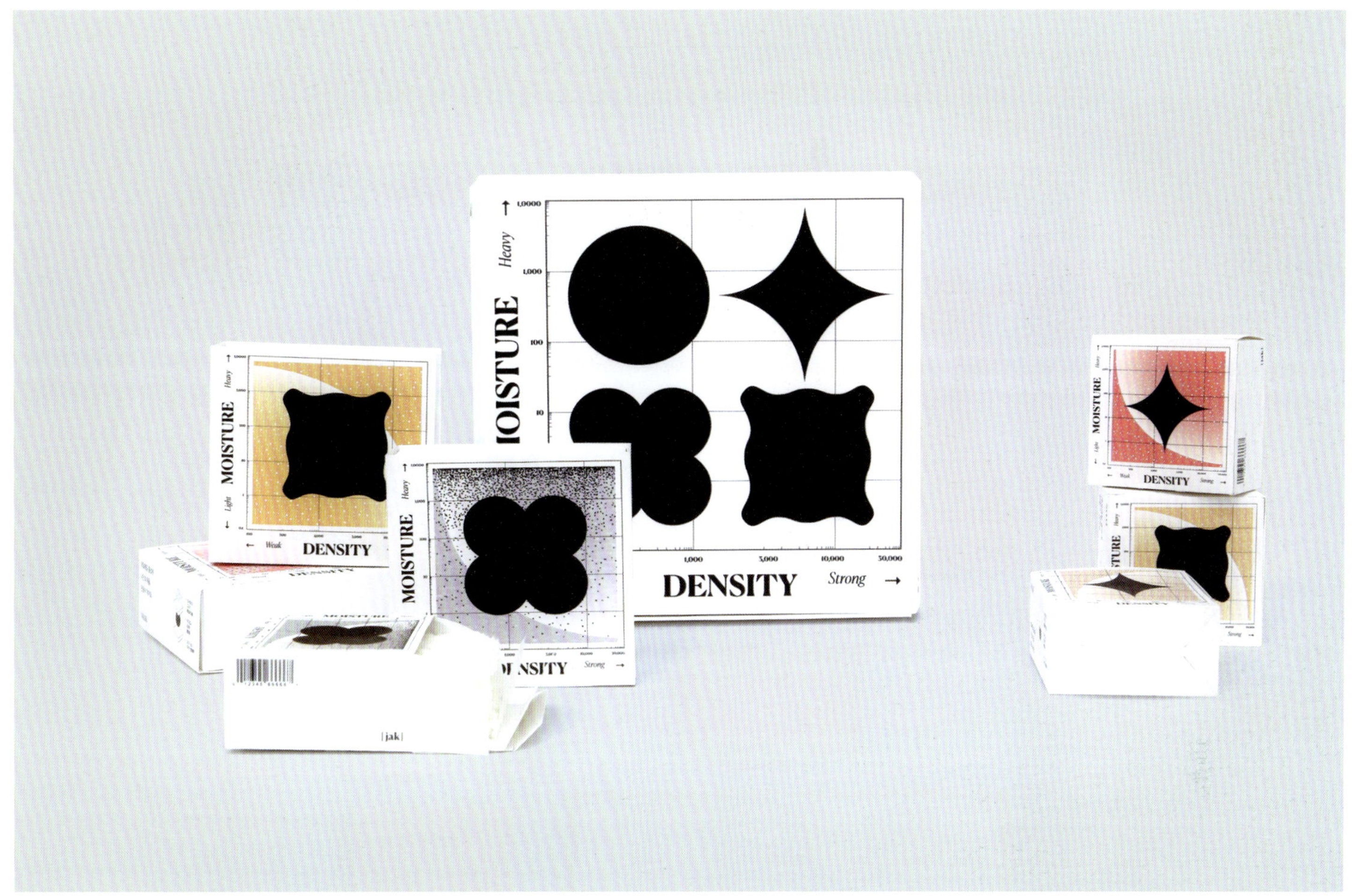

JAK: ENJOY CUSTOMIZING RICE CAKE

D
Eunil Jo, Soyeon Yoon &
Heewon Kim

2008

The graph that shows the degree of toughness and moisture is layered with one color. One main feature is that only one shape with one color of the rice cake should be used in a different single-color package. When an option is selected, graphics and colors change accordingly. Warm colors expressed in the package would maximize the texture of rice cake.
The package uses a fairly wide variety of soft colors and a color is needed to intervene them. Designers used white for the background of the package and black for the graph and pattern to represent the five primary colors without mess.

CAT HATER SURVIVAL KIT

D
Anthony Banks & Melinda Livsey

P
Anthony Banks

2018

Part of the challenge was to create the entire kit for less than $50, which the two designers were able to accomplish by dusting off the old studio art skills and calling in a favor from their local letterpress studio, Porridge Papers. The only thing better than brainstorming the idea for the "Not Sorry" card with the blind hit on "Not" was pulling it off the press and seeing it in person. The screen printing on the box exterior was created using a Yudu Anthony had gathering dust in his basement, and the contents of the box are a combination of inkjet printed hand lettering, Xacto knives, foam core board and various items scouted from corner stores and the internet. The box itself was originally designed to hold wine bottles.

JR EAST WATER BUSINESS 10TH ANNIVERSARY

AD & CD
Minoru Dodo

D
Kazuhiko Hasegawa, Maya Asada &
Ayaka Funata

DS
DODO DESIGN

2016

It is a total production of design related to the 10th anniversary of JR East Water
Business Co., Ltd. establishment.
Launch of new products commemorating the 10th anniversary of company establishment,
opening of anniversary site, present campaign, sampling event...The company made various developments throughout the years.
The designers made ten kinds of packages as commemoration of the 10th anniversary of
mineral water which is a signboard product of JR East Water Business Co., Ltd.
This series of total production was done to convey fun and playfulness to each customer
as a start line for the past 10 years' gratitude and the next decade.

AN NIVER
SA SI RY
TH
10
NCE 2006
Anniv.
A ST
WATER BUSIN ESS
From AQUA Limited 280ml

Happy
EVERYDAY
Came
IT'S SO
Cool
From AQUA Limited 280ml

From AQUA Limited 280ml

Sunday
TUESDAY
WEDNESDAY
FRIDAY
SATURDAY
From AQUA Limited 280ml

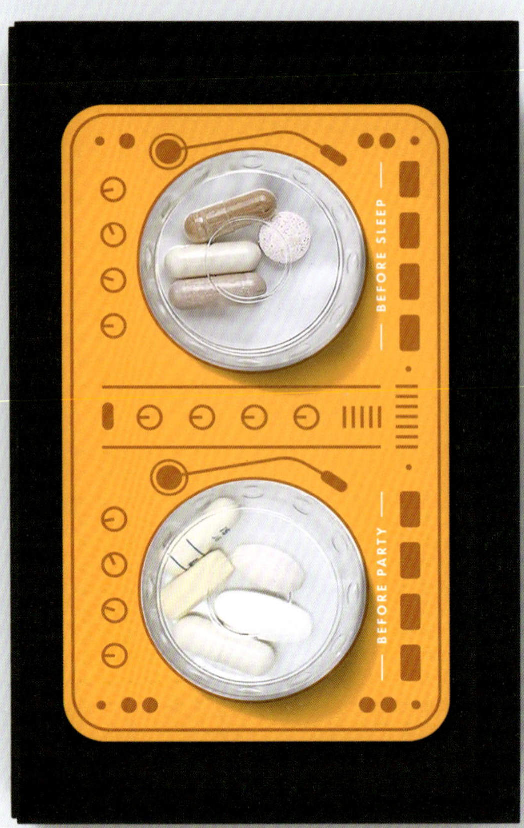

RAVE PACK

D
Ruoxue Wang

DS
Ruoxue Wang

2018

Rave Pack is a unique blend of vitamins and supplements that maximize the experience of raving, dancing and partying, while at the same time making sure you will have the best rest after the party. The packaging utilized the shape of the normal pill pack and combined DJ turntable into the look. So it added more fun and joy to the product itself.

D
Hiné Mizushima

P
Hiné Mizushima

2017

KOGINZASHI EMBROIDERED BROOCH SETS

Hiné Mizushima made these Koginzashi embroidered brooches for the Gift Wrapped 2017 art show at Clutter Gallery in New York. Koginzashi is an embroidery method in a traditional folk needlework from the north of Japan. She used Japanese Kogin embroidery cotton fabric and threads, and tiny Japanese glass beads as well.

THANK YOU IN A CAN

D
Marco Inve

DS
Marco Inve

2018

The project consists of a small batch of cans that Marco designed and sent to all his
clients as a Christmas gift to thank them for the year they just spent together.
Inside the tin cans, they will find a screen printed tote bag with a similar design
to the outside of the cans.
The overall look and feel is inspired by the iconic "Thank you" plastic shopping bag.

Thank
You
Thank you
ありがとう

ROLL CLUB

Roll Club is the food delivery service in Kharkiv, Ukraine. After a couple of years of successful work, they decided to open a little restaurant.

The designers' goal was to make a new identity for the restaurant and delivery. The main challenge was to show the variety of cuisines and dishes and make the new identity in a modern and stylish way. Menu of the delivery includes four cuisines such as Japanese (sushi), Chinese (wok), Italian (pizza, pasta) and American (burgers, fries). That's why the new identity shows that Roll Club is not just about rolls.

The designers decided to create a system of marks that symbolized different countries. For example, they used American pop elements such as stars, strips and reminders about cult characters; symbols of Italy that everyone knows — flag colors and the olive leaves. Specific autographs from Japanese engravings gave them a form for a short texts. China in identity is shown with combination of the red and pink colors and Chinese lanterns.

The company logo demonstrates the union of several kitchens in the menu as well. Tomato symbolizes dishes of Western cuisines since ketchup is a very common ingredient in Italian and American dishes. The fish symbolizes oriental cuisine — Japanese and Chinese. The font part of the logo is enclosed in a frame and superimposed on a sign, like a stamp in Japanese prints.

OUT

AD & CD
Canape Agency

D
Daria Stetsenko

DS
Canape Agency

P
Canape Agency

2018

DS
Nendo

TSUMIKI

P
Akihiro Yoshida

2018

A branding project for a specialist retail securities firm that is part of Marui, a retailer group in Japan.
It specializes in a mutual fund, monthly accumulation scheme. Its appeal is in the easy online application procedure, as well as investments using credit cards which is the first set-up in Japan, and seminars in Marui outlets, intended to open the doors for novice investors without adequate financial literacy.
With a view to reduce the inherent anxiety associated with "finance" and "investment", the investment trust was turned into a physical product, the hypothesis being that the main reason for anxiety was that they are neither visible nor tangible products. The product was therefore formed into a protection charm, inspired by the shape of the Japanese traditional "omamori", so by wearing it in your everyday life or placing it in your living space creates a natural feeling that your future is protected.
The service was named "tsumiki" which means "building blocks" in Japanese. The word also conveys the meaning "tsumi" (accumulation) and "ki" (affection), to portray the sense of growing the asset incrementally month by month, that it is not only the capital accumulating, but also the "affection" is growing stronger.

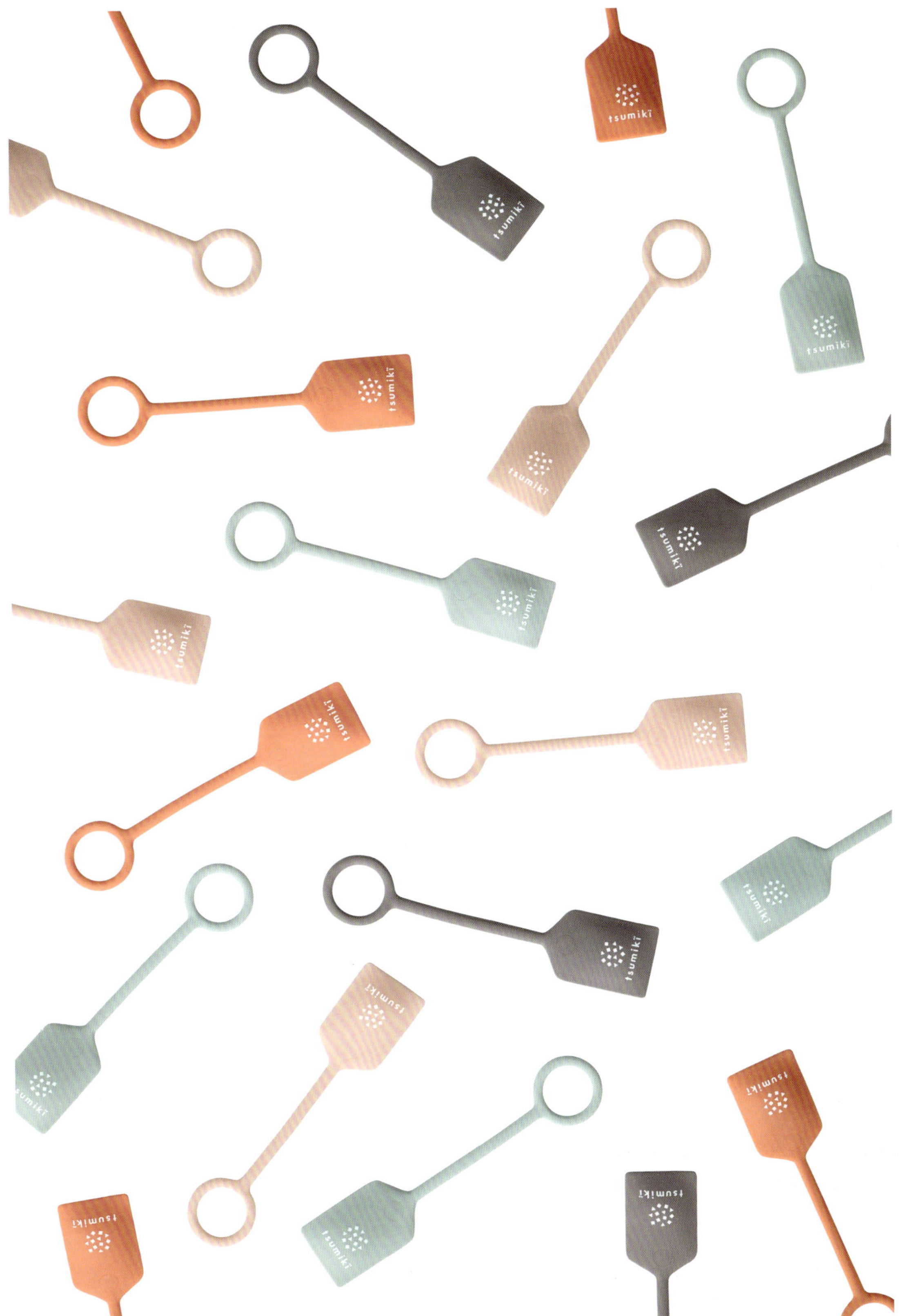

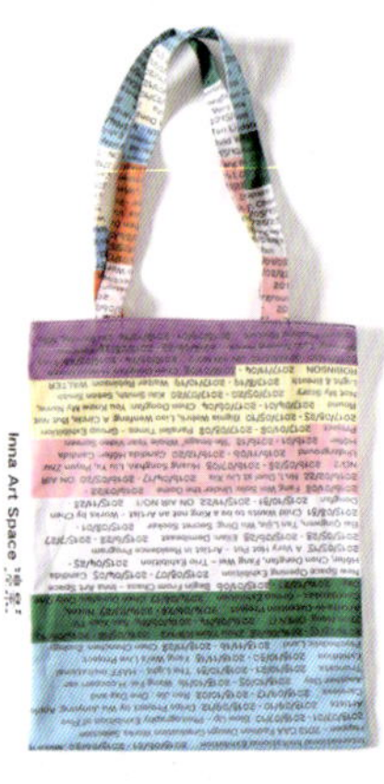 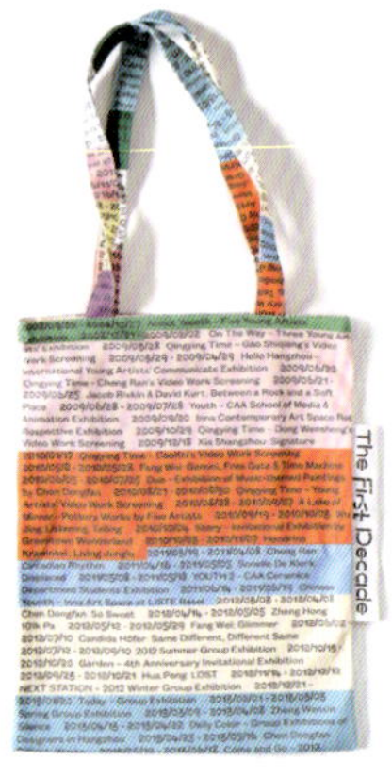  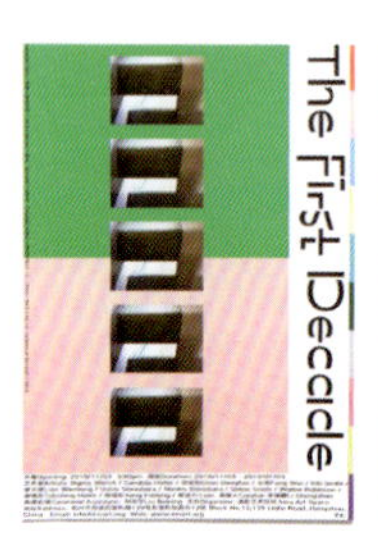 

INNA ART SPACE: THE FIRST DECADE

AD & CD
Qiongjie Lo

D
Qiongjie Lo, Xiaomei Liu, Fan Yang & Cong Chen

DS
TRANSWHITE STUDIO

P
Cong Chen

2018

The project is created for the 10th anniversary of Inna Art Space. The timeline of exhibitions held in the past decade is the main visual element and 10 colors are used to sketch the splendid decade of Inna Art Space. The growth of the Space is demonstrated in an infographic form.

第一个十年   The First Decade

展览前言 / Foreword

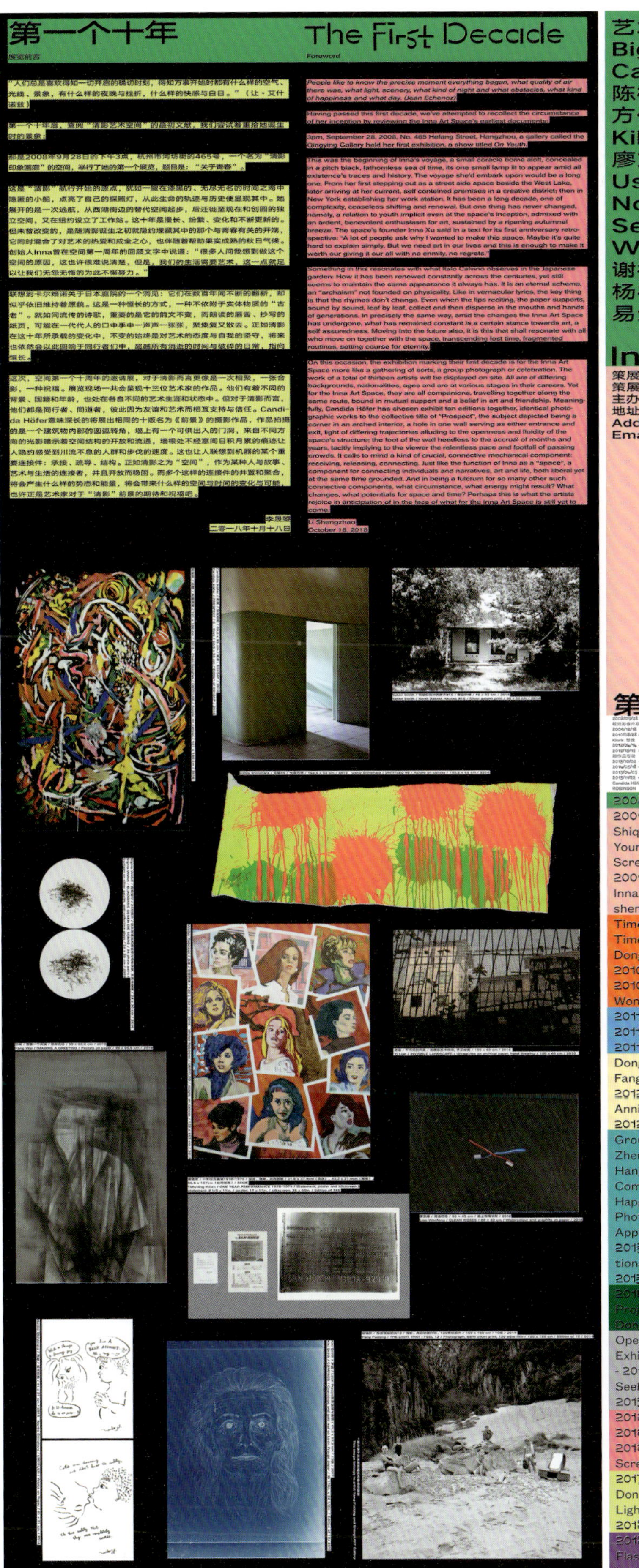

People like to know the precise moment everything began, what quality of air there was, what light, scenery, what kind of night and what obstacles, what kind of happiness and what day. (Jean Echenoz)

Having passed this first decade, we've attempted to recollect the circumstance of her inception by reviewing the Inna Art Space's earliest documents:

3pm, September 28, 2008, No. 465 Hefang Street, Hangzhou, a gallery called the Qingying Gallery held her first exhibition, a show titled *On Youth*.

This was the beginning of Inna's voyage, a small coracle borne aloft, concealed in a pitch black, fathomless sea of time, its one small lamp lit to appear amid all existence's traces and history. The voyage she'd embark upon would be a long one. From her first stepping out as a street side space beside the West Lake, later arriving at her current, self contained premises in a creative district; then in New York establishing her work station. It has been a long decade, one of complexity, ceaseless shifting and renewal. But one thing has never changed, namely, a relation to youth implicit even at the space's inception, admixed with an ardent, benevolent enthusiasm for art, sustained by a ripening autumnal breeze. The space's founder Inna Xu said in a text for its first anniversary retrospective: "A lot of people ask why I wanted to make this space. Maybe it's quite hard to explain simply. But we need art in our lives and this is enough to make it worth our giving it our all with no enmity, no regrets."

Something in this resonates with what Italo Calvino observes in the Japanese garden: How it has been renewed constantly across the centuries, yet still seems to maintain the same appearance it always has. It is an eternal schema, an "archaism" not founded on physicality. Like in vernacular lyrics, the key thing is that the rhymes don't change. Even when the lips reciting, the paper supports, sound by sound, leaf by leaf, collect and then disperse in the mouths and hands of generations. In precisely the same way, amid the changes the Inna Art Space has undergone, what has remained constant is a certain stance towards art, a self assuredness. Moving into the future also, it is this that shall resonate with all who move on together with the space, transcending lost time, fragmented routines, setting course for eternity.

On this occasion, the exhibition marking their first decade is for the Inna Art Space more like a gathering of sorts, a group photograph or celebration. The work of a total of thirteen artists will be displayed on site. All are of differing backgrounds, nationalities, ages and are at various stages in their careers. Yet for the Inna Art Space, they are all companions, travelling together along the same route, bound in mutual support and a belief in art and friendship. Meaningfully, Candida Höfer has chosen exhibit ten editions together, identical photographic works to the collective title of "Prospect", the subject depicted being a corner in an arched interior, a hole in one wall serving as either entrance and exit, light of differing trajectories alluding to the openness and fluidity of the space's structure; the foot of the wall heedless to the accrual of months and years, tacitly implying to the viewer the relentless pace and footfall of passing crowds. It calls to mind a kind of crucial, connective mechanical component: receiving, releasing, connecting. Just like the function of Inna as a "space", a component for connecting individuals and narratives, art and life, both liberal yet at the same time grounded. And in being a fulcrum for so many other such connective components, what circumstance, what energy might result? What changes, what potentials for space and time? Perhaps this is what the artists rejoice in anticipation of in the face of what for the Inna Art Space is still yet to come.

Li Shengzhao
October 18, 2018

艺术家 Artists:
Bignia Wehrli
Candida Höfer
陈栋帆 Chen Dongfan
方伟 Fang Wei
Kiki Smith
廖文峰 Liao Wenfeng
Ushio Shinohara
Noriko Shinohara
Seton Smith
Walter Robinson
谢德庆 Tehching Hsieh
杨福东 Yang Fudong
易连 Yi Lian

The First Decade

Opening: 2018/11/03 3:00pm
Duration: 2018/11/03 – 2019/01/03

Inna Art Space 2008–2018

策展人Curator: 李晟曌 Li Shengzhao
策展助理Curatorial Assistant: 刘呗宁 Liu Beining
主办Organizer: 清影艺术空间 Inna Art Space
地址: 杭州市西湖区留和路139号东信和创园内12栋
Address: Block No.12,139 Liuhe Road, Hangzhou, China
Email: info@innart.org   Web: www.innart.org

第一个十年   清影

2008/09/28 - 2008/10/27 About Younth – Five Young Artists' Exhibition   2008/12/21 - 2009/02/02 On The Way – Three Young Artists' Exhibition   2009/03/28 Qingying Time – Gao Shiqiang's Video Work Screening   2009/03/29 - 2009/04/29 Hello Hangzhou – International Young Artists' Communicate Exhibition   2009/06/20 Qingying Time - Cheng Ran's Video Work Screening   2009/06/21 - 2009/06/25 Jacob Rivkin & David Kurt: Between a Rock and a Soft Place   2009/06/28 - 2009/07/28 Youth – CAA School of Media & Animation Exhibition   2009/09/20 Inna Contemporary Art Space Ret Rospective Exhibition   2009/10/29 Qingying Time – Dong Wensheng's Video Work Screening   2009/12/18 Xia Shangzhou: Signature   2010/01/17 Qingying Time – CaoKai's Video Work Screening   2010/05/8 - 2010/05/28 Fang Wei: Gemini, Free Gate & Time Machine   2010/06/05 - 2010/07/05 Duo – Exhibition of Music-themed Paintings by Chen Dongfan   2010/08/21 - 2010/08/30 Qingying Time – young artists' Video Work Screening   2010/08/28 - 2010/09/07 A Lake of Mirror - Pottery Works by Five Artists   2010/09/19 - 2010/10/03 Wu Jing: Listening, Telling   2010/10/04 Story – Invitational Exhibition by Greentown Wonderland   2010/10/23 - 2010/11/07 Hendrina Krawinkel: Living Jungle   2011/03/19 - 2011/04/08 Cheng Ran: Circadian Rhythm   2011/04/16 - 2011/05/05 Sonelle De Klerk: Displaced   2011/05/8 - 2011/05/18 YOUTH 2 - CAA Ceramics Department Students' Exhibition   2011/06/14 - 2011/06/19 Chinese Younth – Inna Art Space at LISTE Basel   2012/03/03 - 2012/04/08 Chen Dongfan: So Sweet   2012/04/14 - 2012/05/05 Zheng Hong: 101k Pa   2012/05/12 - 2012/05/29 Fang Wei: Glimmer   2012/06/02 - 2012/07/10 Candida Höfer: Same Different, Different Same   2012/07/12 - 2012/09/10 2012 Summer Group Exhibition   2012/10/13 - 2012/10/20 Garden – 4th Anniversary Invitational Exhibition   2012/09/25 - 2012/10/21 Hua Peng: LOET   2012/11/14 - 2012/12/12 NEXT STATION – 2012 Winter Group Exhibition   2012/12/21 - 2013/01/20 Today – Group Exhibition   2013/02/01 - 2013/03/08 Spring Group Exhibition   2013/03/09 - 2013/04/08 Zheng Wenxin: Silence   2013/04/13 - 2013/04/22 Daily Color – Group Exhibitions of Designers in Hangzhou   2013/04/25 - 2013/05/16 Chen DongfanRcent: Works   2013/05/19 - 2013/06/08 Come and Go – 2013 International Invitational Exhibition   2013/06/21 - 2013/06/30 Make It Happen – 2013 CAA Fashion Design Graduation Works Selection   2013/07/01 - 2013/07/10 Blow Up – Photography Exhibition of Five Artists   2013/09/10 - 2013/09/12 Drips Project by Wu Junyong: Apple Careless   2013/09/17 - 2013/10/02 Ren Jie: One Day and Another Day   2013/10/05 - 2013/10/15 Wang Fei: H.cooperi var Truncata   2013/10/21 - 2013/10/31 The Light – HAFF Invitational Exhibtion   2013/10/30 - 2013/11/18 Fang Wei's Live Project: Psychedelic Land   2013/11/16 - 2013/11/28 Chen Chenchen: Zoology   2014/03/15 - 2014/04/15 Zhou Yilun: R3PM3   2014/03/15 - 2014/06/10 Zhen Hong: OPEN IT   2014/06/14 - 2014/06/24 San Xian TV: Artists-in-Detention Project   2014/06/28 - 2014/07/27 Notes, Coordinates – Group Exhibition   2014/11/08 - 2014/12/27 Chen Dongfan: Only One Day   2015/01/06 Begin From Chaos – Inna Art Space New Space Opening Exhibition   2015/03/07 - 2015/04/05 Candida Höfer, Chen Dongfan, Fang Wei – Tri Exhibition   2015/04/25 - 2015/05/15 A Very Hot Pot – Artist in Residence Program   2015/05/23 - 2015/06/23 Elian: Demibeast   2015/6/28 - 2015/7/27 Bai Qingwen, Tan Lijie, Wu Ding: Secret Seeker   2015/08/01 - 2015/08/31 Child Wants to be a King not an Artist – Works by Chen Dongfan   2015/10/31 - 2015/11/22 ON AIR NO/1   2015/11/28 - 2016/01/03 Fang Wei Solo: Under the Dome   2016/01/22 - 2016/02/22 No.1, Duel at Liu Xia   2016/04/17 - 2016/05/20 ON AIR NO/2   2016/05/28 - 2016/07/03 Huang Songhao, Liu Ya, Payen Zhu: Underground   2016/11/06 - 2016/12 Candida Höfer: Candida Höfer   2016/01 - 2016/12 "Re-Image" Whole Year Video Screen Project   2017/01/08 - 2017/03/08 Parallel Times – Group Exhibition   2017/03/25 - 2017/05/10 Bignia Wehrli, Liao Wenfeng: A Circle, But Not Round   2017/04/01 - 2017/06/04 Chen Dongfan: You Know My Name, Not My Story   2017/05/20 - 2017/07/20 Kiki Smith, Seton Smith: Light & Breath   2017/8/19 - 2017/10/19 Walter Robinson: WALTER ROBINSON   2017/11/04 - 2018/01/03 Chen Dongfan: Heated Bloom   2018/01/20 - 2018/03/10 ON AIR NO/3   2018/03/24 - 2018/05/23 Liao Wenfeng: Eyes Moving Pencil   2018/06/23 - 2018/08/12 Fangwei: Fangwei Flashing Restart   2018/09/01 - 2018/10/14 Liu Beining, Milo Wang: G train, L train

Brandirection®

Civilian Art Stage

People's cultural life has been growing increasingly abundant and with this trend, creative design markets have also emerged with growing popularity. Creative design markets usually feature people displaying and selling original handmade works and collections in a specific place. It is a communication mode arising in the evolvement of the creative industry, focusing on building open and diversified creative environments and trading platforms for the wide variety of emerging designers and artists. These events advocate individual creation and innovation, and encourage entrepreneurship with creative businesses, with an emphasis on providing cultural added value besides the practical value of products or services of cultural, artistic and design nature. We can say that creative design markets are an experimental platform to ignite creativity and commercialize creative works.

Generally speaking, with low barriers to entry, the events are more like a civilian art stage. So the forms of works are more diversified and a larger range of target can be reached. Apart from work display, they also include lectures, mini concerts, street performances, screenings, creative competitions and workshops. Maintaining the theme on various concrete forms of original culture, creative design markets become carnivalesque parties for young people.

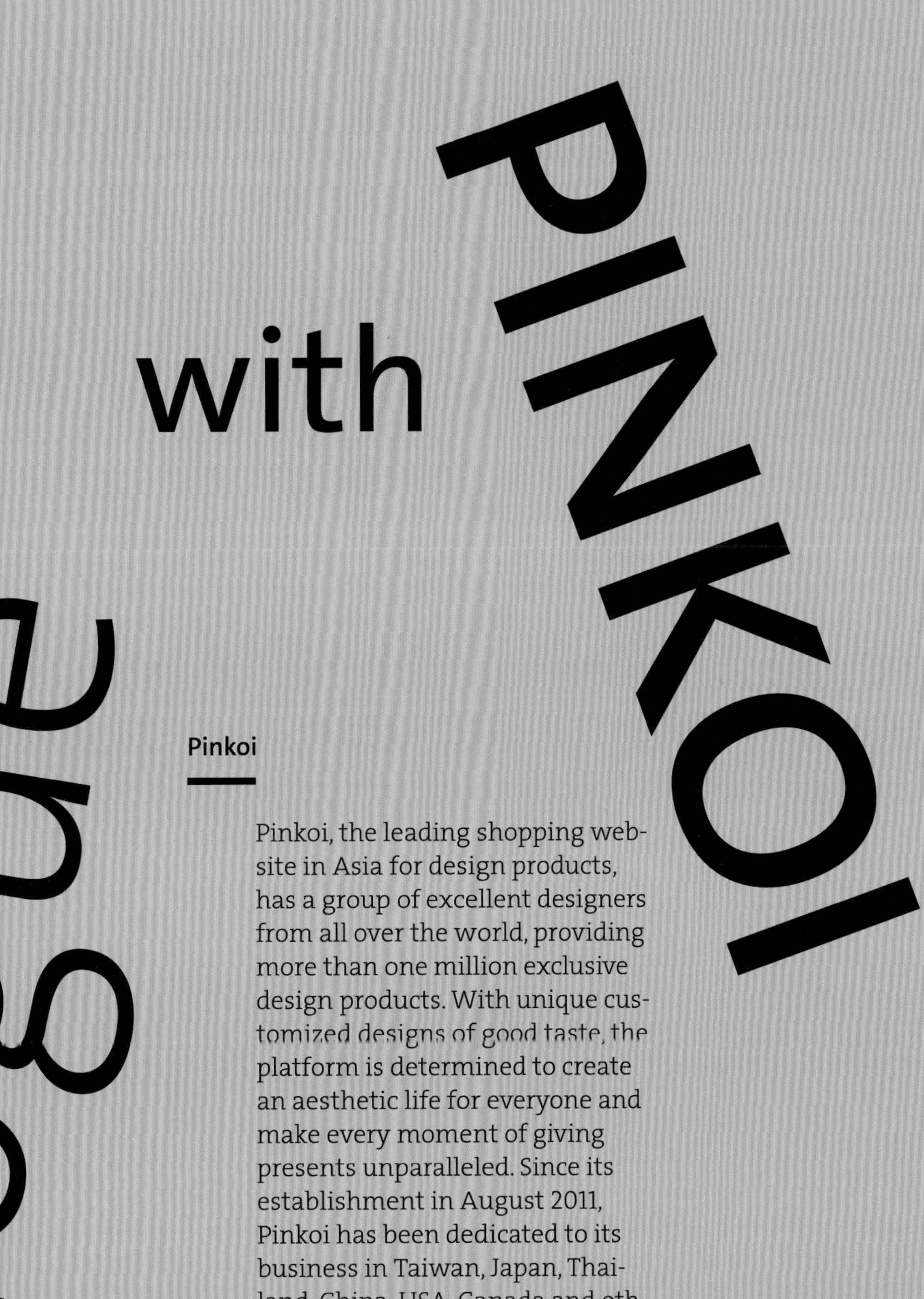

Pinkoi

Pinkoi, the leading shopping website in Asia for design products, has a group of excellent designers from all over the world, providing more than one million exclusive design products. With unique customized designs of good taste, the platform is determined to create an aesthetic life for everyone and make every moment of giving presents unparalleled. Since its establishment in August 2011, Pinkoi has been dedicated to its business in Taiwan, Japan, Thailand, China, USA, Canada and other international markets, in hope to make Asian's fascinating good designs glow all over the world and create a design ecosphere for better life.
https://pinkoi.com

The evolvement of internet technology has expanded to cover every industry and permeate every aspect of our life. It then resulted in the emergence of electronic commerce (e-commerce). And now people are getting more and more accustomed to the convenience of shopping online. Almost anything is available in online shopping malls, surely with no exception for creative commodities. It was at this right moment that Pinkoi, the Taiwan design shopping website for design products, was born. The website was built in 2011 with a white background and square blocks, simple yet pleasant. The platform adopts a verification system to sell original Asian design products,and charges transaction management fees after the products have been sold.

Pinkoi aims to create a global brand. Over the years, it has been ceaselessly expanding the scope of commodities and services. It first collaborated with Japanese designers, along with cooperation with other Asian designers, and then expands to markets of Beijing and Shanghai. Now Pinkoi has 12,000 active design shops and more than 10,000 designers from Taiwan and all over the world. With this resource pool, Pinkoi made the decision to go offline and began to hold Pinkoi markets. Moreover, it recently made another two new attempts in offline experiential courses and physical pop-up stores.

Editor
Virginia Ruan

Creative Design Market Alive from Online

Interviewer
Virginia Ruan

It has been significant to create for consumers unique memories with experience.

Last Christmas, Pinkoi hosted a Pinkoi Market in Taipei. When did you start to run the market? Pinkoi started off as an online original commodity shopping platform, so what impelled you to organize offline markets?
We started our first Christmas market in 2015, with everything curated and organized by ourselves. The fascination of each design stems from the passionate and talented creator behind it. That is why we hoped to build O2O(online to offline) connections through entity market events at the very beginning, allowing designers to step down from online to interactively communicate face to face with consumers. In this way, consumers can see the actual commodities in person and moreover, feel the love and perseverance of designers towards creation through actual interactions.

Do you come up with different themes for every session of the market? How do you usually curate for the event?
The theme of a market determines the direction and key of the entire activity, as well as its target participants. Therefore, the planning of a theme is very significant. While planning for a market, we select and explore the theme according to local cultures, local people's favors and topics of concern. Involvement with people and designers who pay attention to the theme always create more possibilities.
For example, when we were planning the market in Japan last year, we found people there are paying increasingly close attention to Taiwan. So we decided on the theme of"Taiwanese Zakka"and hosted a market in hand with Hanshin Department Store which turned out to be a great success. In Taiwan, we discovered that selecting

and giving gifts is the most heated topic in the end of a year. Hence we adopted Christmas as the theme, integrating designs from all over Asia from the perspective of public demands, so as to make know the good designs in Asia.

At Pinkoi, we have a project team dedicated for market curation, in which the manager leads the cross-department team to work collaboratively. They would first make a plan according to the event objectives, atmosphere and scale of the site, and theme. Then come the booth registration and conceptions for onsite activities to enrich the event. One conception is designer workshops to go with the market, where consumers can enjoy the fun of DIY in person.

Is there any change in the variety of original design brands over the years?

Yes, we can see a growing maturity in Asian original design commodities, and more designers are absorbing local cultural nutrients into their commercial creations. With a more diversified range of materials, a lot of amazing creative themes are often dug out. Besides this, we have been taking in more categories. Illustration and paper design, as usual, is the ordinary category. But a more diversified scheme is now accessible, covering clothing with accessories, home supplies, tea, desserts etc. We are absolutely seeing the overwhelming power of Asian design creativity.

In 2018, Pinkoi expanded its event scale to cover 5 Asian cities. Do you adopt a registration system for participation or invite vendors to participate? Any entry criteria? And do you encounter any problem in original brand recruitment?

The mission of Pinkoi is to help talented designers and

creators succeed. So basically we send the information to the designers on our online shopping platform and they register to participate. Markets are popular these years and they are enthusiastic in our events. Our market would always attract large crowds of designers who have already been selling their creations on our website. Normally, any designer of our online platform with a certain quantity of commodities can register to participate in our markets.

Apart from offline markets, Pinkoi initiated Pinkoi School last July. Can you tell us about it? What role is it playing in your strategic integration of online and offline resources?
We are conscious of the fact that the experience economy will be the next trend. Under the current circumstance that most people are wild about uniform scenic spots, shooting angles and trended commodities, it has been significant to create for consumers unique memories with experience. And this is exactly the original purpose with which Pinkoi started our school. We hope that besides shopping on Pinkoi, they can have their own special commodities and memories via interaction with the creators, so as to fully achieve our brand vision of helping consumers lead aesthetic lives with good designs.
By now Pinkoi school has held workshops like fragrant candle workshop, lettering workshop, dried wreath making workshop and half-day tour in tea gardens.

In dozens of European cities, creative design markets have become part of their charm. Cosmopolises like London, Paris, Tokyo and Milan have their own creative design markets. These events are the starting points for emerging designers and artists to set up their own businesses. These markets meet modern city people's, especially the younger generation's need and eagerness to seek and explore in an open and multifold creative ecology. Those young people who have creativity to sell would always opt for these events to start off. Here *BranD* would like to introduce two design markets in Asia and Europe: Market of Artists And Designers (MAAD) organized by Red Dot Design Museum Singapore and Milan Design Market. Having been running for at least several years, these two markets are growing in both size and influence with their mature operation patterns. Just keep reading to find out more.

Editor
Virginia Ruan

Starting Points for Creativity Business

Dialogue with

MILAN DESIGN MARKET

Milan Design Market

Milan Design Market is a space dedicated to emerging designers and brands, who can exhibit and sell their creations, but also network and develop new business opportunities during Milan Design Week since 4 years ago. It's also an online platform where you can "get the WOW" through the e-store and be updated about design trends on the blog.

Interviewer
Virginia Ruan

This mixture of cultures and influences can be appreciated.

Milan Design Market is a space where emerging designers and brands could exhibit and sell their creations. When was it initiated, and what motivated the team to start the event?
Milan Design Market is one of our first projects that we have launched as Blankhub.com. Being a creative studio based in Milan and doing many projects related to world of design, we have realised during Milan Design Week there were not many affordable collectives with a great selections of emerging designers and design studios. So 4 years ago we said let's create one, where we embrace great design! And Milan Design Market became one of the most followed events of Milan Design Week and now we also have our e-store and blog to give more exposure to designers in our community all year long.

What sections does the event include? Do you have any specific theme for each section and how do you determine it?
The general installation of the event is changing every year; our host architects are creating 3 dimensional feels like drawings in 1:1 scale in order to make visitors feel inside them! Last year we have made our first comprehensive exhibition with different imaginary spaces created, by Dutch architect Sven Jansse, instead this year the name of the concept will be "Finding the lost city". Once visitors enter in the space, they will discover a new city that they haven't seen before. Other new experiences for this year will be through the Aria application — visitors will be able to access a series of augmented reality content, to find out more about the products on display and on the theme itself, surpassing the boundary of the physical space.

Apart from the general installation we have two different options for our participating designers: they can have their individual stands to showcase their products or they can take part in our pop-up store with their products. In both options we have a central cashier where we make the sales of the products. That makes everything easy for international participants. Milan Design Market is one of the only design exhibition during Milan Design Week where you can also buy what you see!

How do you see the products displayed at the event? Any change in variety, originality or quality over these years?
We always aimed to have designers from all over the world with common design aesthetics as ours. The products we had in our exhibition should be innovative either in the materials or in the design. At the beginning, we didn't have as much as applications as we have now!
After four years as Milan Design Market, we have exhibitors from all over the world for real. Last year among 1,000 applications we handpicked the most interesting projects and we went to other design weeks to scout undiscovered designers. We met with incredible minds. We had projects from Japan, Mexico, Korea, Iran, France, Mauritius, Netherlands, US etc. The variation of different perspectives makes our event super interesting.

What's the entry criteria for vendors participating in the market?
We don't have a specific criteria. The important thing is to bring something new to the market. We don't exhibit just final products—it can be even just a design idea or prototype.

What do you think of the creative environment in Milan or even Italy?
Italy, without a doubt is the Mecca of design and can be great opportunity for creatives, since the establishment of the first furniture makers fair more than 100 years ago, thanks to that Milan became the go to place for all the latest trends and production techniques. It allows the city a constant flow of ideas, gathering the best designers from every corner of the world; this mixture of cultures and influences can be appreciated. Besides all the good things Milan has to offer, we still face the problem of rigid institutions and the established companies that gather the most attention. Unfortunately, most of the time they are not as dynamic and innovative as emerging creatives.

What sector of design are you interested in? Why?
We are interested in design in 360 degrees; it can be product design as well as sound design, food design or light design etc. At the moment we are not selecting fashion products for our exhibition because we believe there are many events out there for fashion designers where for others it is very limited. Instead on our e-store we would like to have emerging fashion designers' works as well as other designers'!

Elvin Seah

MAAD (Market of Artists And Designers) is hosted by the Red Dot Design Museum Singapore, and Elvin is the organizer.
He is also responsible for the communications work for the museum and design award.

Interviewer
Virginia Ruan

As evening approaches, the museum transforms into the only night showcase for local designers and artists to feature original works.

MAAD is presented as a creative marketplace of artists, designers, craftsmen, artisans, creators and brand owners, focusing on original works. It was initiated in July 2006. What motivated the team to start the event?
MAAD began as a test-bed for enterprising creatives to showcase their original works and talents, as a contact point to test-market the viability of the creative ideas of passionate and enterprising artists, and nurture the local enterprising community.
As a marketplace, it comes with low barriers of entry (in terms of retail commitment and rent) for the local community to test market and showcase their works. There is a gap in the market back in 2006, and MAAD then became the pioneer in creating a space for the local creative community to gather, test market and showcase their works.
Joining MAAD only requires 1 night commitment, and that fees begin at $50 as compared to the usual retail space terms.

What sections does the event include? Do you have any specific theme for each section and how do you determine it?
The event is hosted at the Red Dot Design Museum Singapore as part of its on-going efforts to invigorate the creative environment in Singapore. As evening approaches, the museum transforms into the only night showcase for local designers and artists to feature original works, creative workshops against the backdrop of the design museum and its permanent design exhibitions.

How do you see the products displayed at the event? Any change in variety, originality or quality over these years?
The majority of vendors work with accessories and handmade zakka. Over the years, people have started to accept art markets as a safe place to showcase their works and the market have started attracting talents with a more diverse interest including leather works, shoemaking, perfume making, self-produced cosmetic brushes, illustrations etc. Because of the nature of the market, there are vendors who have been doing the same craft for over 10 years, and there are also new up and coming teams experimenting and trying out if their ideas will work.

What's the entry criteria for vendors participating in the market?
All items presented must be original works. They don't have to be 100% produced or hand made by the creator, but there must be some form of input/ownership in it, i.e. designed, drawn, prototyped or conceptualised by the creator or by the team. We do not curate who has more creative works, but thought it is only fair to let the market decide. As long as they are original works, all creators should get the chance to share what they have with the public.

What do you think of the creative environment in Singapore?
The local community's entrepreneurial intent is growing with an increase in MAAD participation over the years from 20-30 vendors each session to an average of 60. I would think that indie retailers, speciality stores, local independent labels and its related scene are about to stay in people's mindshare in the next few years or so.
On a macro level, good design is also made conscious by the Singapore government especially after being identified in Singapore's Design Masterplan. The presence of the Red Dot Design Museum in Singapore also contributes to this consciousness in terms of aspirations for design excellence on the world stage. This means that the creative work have not stopped.

What sector of design are you interested in? Why?
Because of the nature of my work, I have been brewing a liking for product design and its processes. We have been striving for perfection in the things we do, such that even in our everyday problems, it has become a habit for me to approach them as if they were part of a design process waiting to be made conscious. I believe it is this approach that will be able to uplift ourselves to be better.

People usually say cartoon is a privilege for children, but I think adults need it more. Modern people living in metropolises all have emotions and moods with nowhere to place, however glamorous and ambitious they may appear. When the entire world has become sophisticated, deep inside people still keep a corner for childlike innocence, which is a vent for most of them to deal with stress. It has already been well demonstrated by the overwhelming popularity of the animated cartoon series Peppa Pig enchanting people of all ages, and the rubber duck travelling around the world alluring a flood of fans. The healing effects brought about by these cute cartoon characters are amazing. They are an effective medicine for the stressful people who retain a childish heart.

The innocence of cartoon images can rescue the exhausted adults out of reality. Immersed in the cartoon dream, they can relive the pleasure and joy in childhood, back to their original minds. It needs not be a very exquisite image or acting cute all the time. It can be a funny fellow imbued with ordinary people's longing and truthfulness like a smiling Shiba Inu. RICHWANT is a celebrated cartoon Shiba Inu in China, originally created by a top Chinese design team. Born in December 2017, this Shiba Inu with a gold ingot on its head prides itself on its owner – the god of wealth. This cute image has been endowed with the traits of talent and fortune to bring people good luck. It is also quite humanized with a zest for food, so a series of 34 illustrations about it tasting food in 34 provinces and cities in China has been created. Since its birth, RICHWANT's lovely image has made it a star among the young, enjoying a remarkably high popularity on all social platforms. Currently the cartoon image has gained a fan group totaling about 2 million and appeared in diverse exhibition and offline activities, winning a good reputation in domestic cartoon industry. In addition, its team offers IP planning design and ecological chain development services. RICHWANT hammers at a top domestic original cartoon IP. The creation of the image, however, is just the beginning. Long-term development and maintenance are indispensable to deliver fresh contents for its tender shoot to grow. The fresh and bold attempt of RICH ART SHOW can yet be regarded as a diverting art exhibition.

The show invited more than 50 domestic artists and designers in various fields to make trans-disciplinary creations. Every guest depicted the image of RICHWANT with their own ideas and artistic features in a hand-making way, sparkling diversified inspirations and creativity.

Editor
Catherin Huang

Live a Simple Life with Much Fun

RICHWANT

全国50+
先锋艺术家"柴艺"展
RICH ART SHOW

主办方 汪柴主动漫
协办方 LOGO大师 赫式 潮尚季
地 点 上海大悦城
媒 体 今日头条、新浪微博、广州平面设计师联盟、顶尖包装、搜狐、网易、名车志、芒果TV、爱奇艺、湖南卫视、世界时装之莞ELLE

2018 12/06 有创意"柴"敢变
汪柴主
RICH WANT

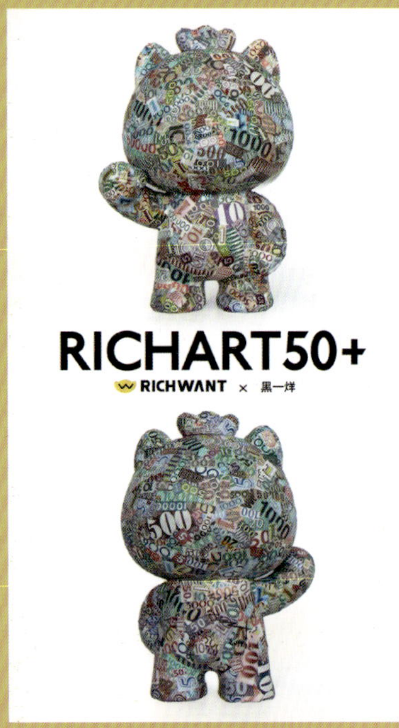

In the creation, RICHWANT is a blank piece of paper for the artists and designers to chuck on the color of their choices. So how did they reshape it? Three of the artists and designers shared their experiences with *BranD*.

Yiyang Hei, founder of SenseTeam, said he felt lucky to have the opportunity to appreciate diversified creations under the same theme which broadened his dimension of thinking. He blended the motif of gaming with his own matured IP of "money scheme", and integrated the global currency values with new media IPs, contrasting the serious social subject with RICHWANT's entertaining image to redefine it. Tiger Pan, the industry "craftsman" with aesthetic spirits and commercial values, is most spellbound by the humanized setting of RICHWANT tempting him to recreate its image. With the embellishment of traditional Chinese elements, he injected a self-personality to RICHWANT and turned it into a strong tiger possessing sharp claws and eyes as well as cuteness representing by the tail-wagging doggy pattern on its chest, its small and round nose, and the horn-like hat. Artist Weicong Deng created a rather "Cantonese" RICHWANT. Each creation is a challenge for him. Deng told us, "At the beginning, I hoped to create a transparent effect for the entire head except the five sense organs but found it really difficult. So I hollowed the positions for eyes which turned out to be satisfying. What I am trying to say is creating is actually a really interesting process. Sometimes only when we set to do it, will we find out it's not what we thought it was. And this problem-solving process is also very important for the creator himself."

The creations at RICH ART SHOW were all handmade. Aaron He, creative director of RICHWANT, revealed that they hoped people can participate in handmade project activities, exerting their acqierement to express their ideas under the theme. Also, the team hopes this show will spread to the whole nation allowing more young and middle-aged people, even people from all social ranks to participate, to achieve their goal of art popularization and communication.

To attract more youngsters who like Shiba Inus, the team has made RICHWANT a super internet celebrity. Apart from the maturing RICH ART SHOW, theme convenience stores are another breakthrough. The stores provide fun space for 24-hour food and amusements with its slogan "Live a Simple Life with Much Fun". They adopt the concept of "say no to a too complicated life" to advocate a young and simple lifestyle. The team underlines this platform and will initiate collaborations in a lot more cities. In their plan, their convenience stores will represent rich and diverting scenes according to settings of communities, office buildings and shopping malls. They believe these interesting stores will bring about more joyful and happy experience to people's life.

Moreover, the creation of an IP image inevitably needs derivative development. So RICHWANT has its own pool of derivative products for its fans and provides customized services as well. In future, they will also cooperate with suppliers to develop products for different fields. One thing to be expected is RICHWANT's new book *RICHWANT's Diary* will be published this March.

The suffocating fast pace of modern life makes people long for simple innocence. By activating the concept of "Living a Simple Life with Much Fun", the cute RICHWANT expects to build a cozy fun space for modern people who loves cuddling cartoon.

Brandream®

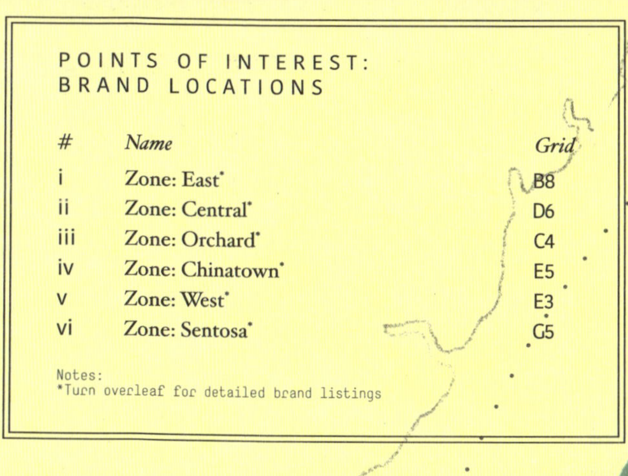

Singapore

Noun

(i) an island on the Strait of Singapore, off the 'S' tip of the Malay Peninsula.

(ii) an independent republic comprising this island and a few adjacent islets: member of the Commonwealth of Nations; formerly a British crown colony (1946–59) and member of the federation of Malaysia (1963–65). 220 sq. mi. (570 sq. km). *Capital*: Singapore.

(iii) a seaport in and the capital of this republic.

Related forms
singaporean, noun, adjective

BRAND
Singapore

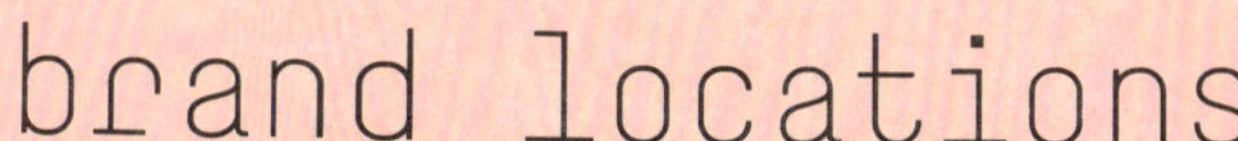

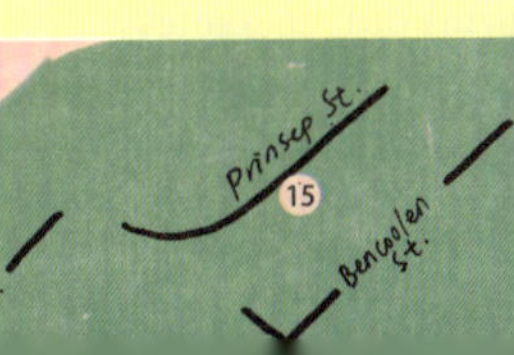

GUIDE : Edition

[1] **Super Loco** ▲
60 Robertson Quay

[2] **Yoga Movement** ⅄
31A & 33A New Bridge Road

[11] **Basheer Graphic Books** ●
Bras Basah Complex #04-19

[12] **National Museum of Singapore** ⅄
93 Stamford Road

LEGEND:

▲ EAT ● SHOP ⅄ PLAY ◆ STAY ■ WORK ★ MRT

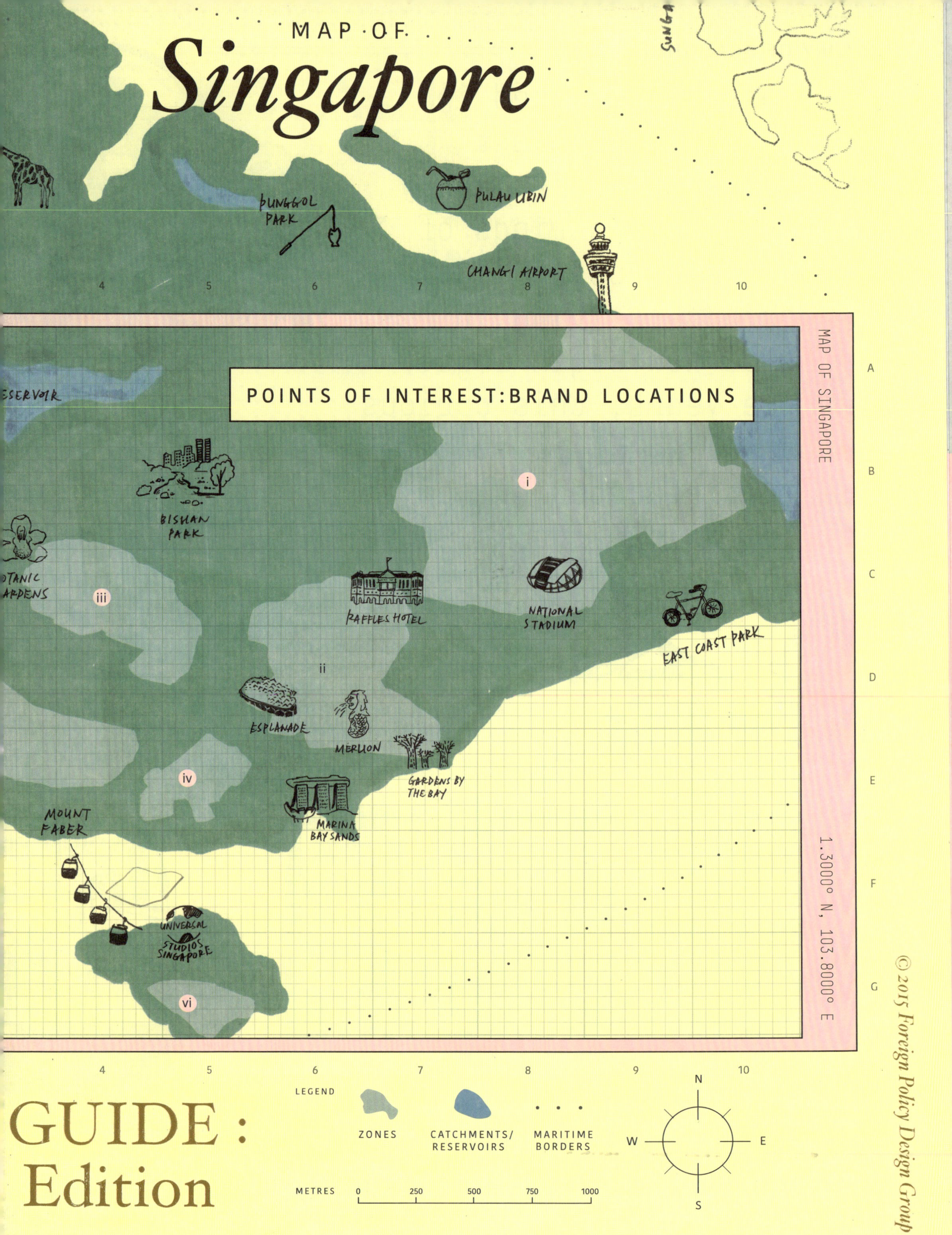

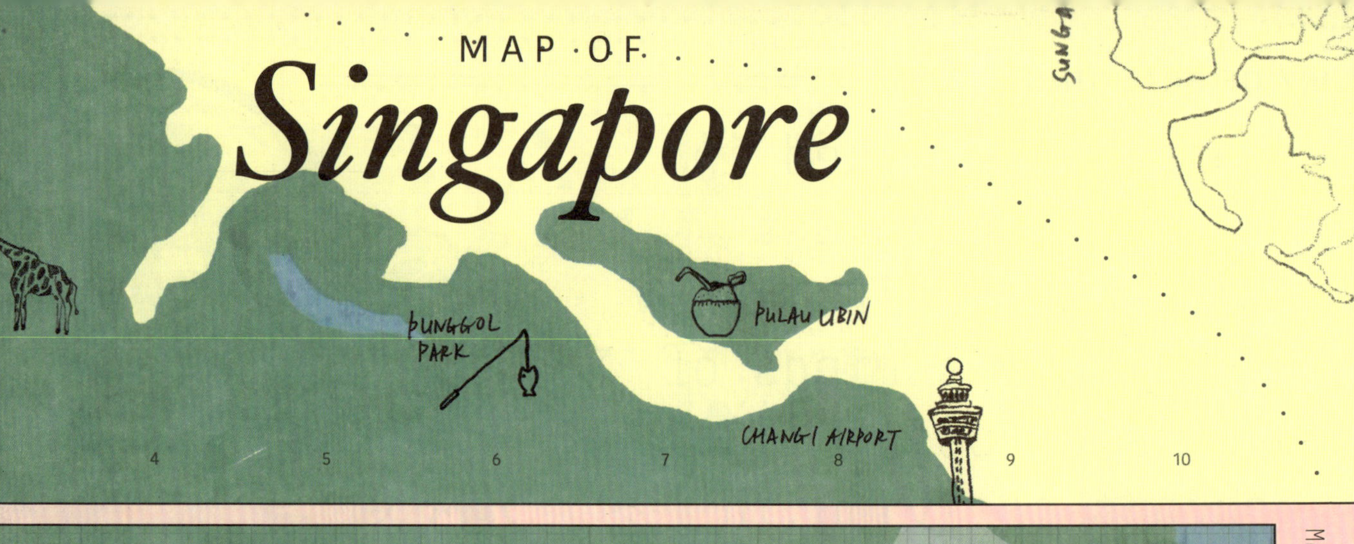

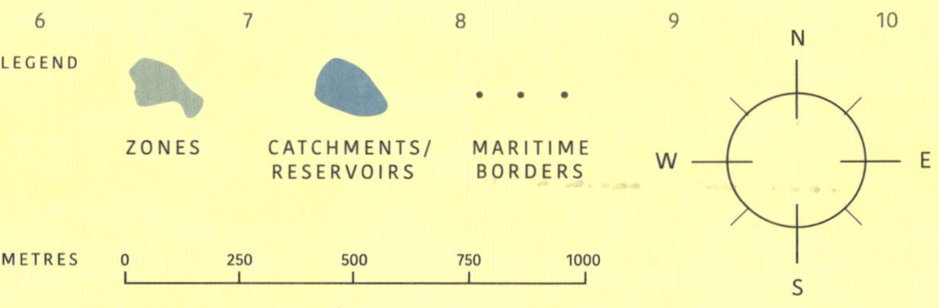

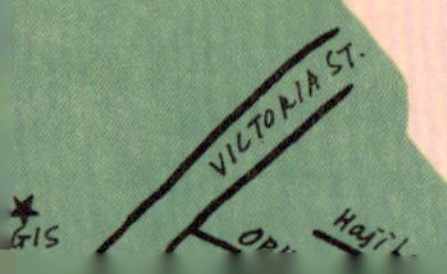